First Steps

PowerPoint 2000

Teresa Adams

Stella Smith

Georgia Perimeter College

THE DRYDEN PRESS
HARCOURT BRACE COLLEGE PUBLISHERS

Fort Worth Philadelphia San Diego New York Orlando Austin San Antonio
Toronto Montreal London Sydney Tokyo

EXECUTIVE EDITOR *Christina A. Martin*
MARKET STRATEGIST *Debbie K. Anderson*
DEVELOPMENTAL EDITOR *Larry Crowder*
PROJECT EDITOR *Christy Goldfinch*
ART DIRECTOR *Scott Baker*
PRODUCTION MANAGER *Eddie Dawson*

Cover illustration by Steven Lyons

ISBN: 0-03-026142-2
Library of Congress Catalog Card Number: 99-61511

Portions of this work were previously published.

Screen shots of Microsoft® PowerPoint used by permission of Microsoft Corporation.

Address for domestic orders:
The Dryden Press, 6277 Sea Harbor Drive, Orlando, FL 32887-6777
1-800-782-4479

Address for international orders:
International Customer Service
The Dryden Press, 6277 Sea Harbor Drive, Orlando, FL 32887-6777
407-345-3800
(fax) 407-345-4060
(e-mail) hbintl@harcourtbrace.com

Address for editorial correspondence:
The Dryden Press, 301 Commerce Street, Suite 3700, Fort Worth, TX 76102

Web site address:
http://www.hbcollege.com

Printed in the United States of America

9 0 1 2 3 4 5 6 7 8 751 9 8 7 6 5 4 3 2 1

The Dryden Press
Harcourt Brace College Publishers

PREFACE

Your first steps in learning a new computer program should help you become productive quickly. This manual accomplishes that goal by showing you how to create the most common PowerPoint 2000 documents.

These first steps must also be easy to follow. PowerPoint 2000 is a powerful program with so many features that it would be easy for a new student to become lost in its complexity. This manual is easy to follow because of its simple organization and consistent placement of instructions and figures.

The steps you should follow are only on left-hand pages; the figures showing how your screen should look are only on right-hand pages. If your screen doesn't match the appropriate figure, it's easy to retrace the steps until you get it right. In addition, annotations on the figures point out menus, buttons, and other objects required to follow the steps.

Throughout these lessons, you will also find additional helpful information in the form of Tips, Notes and Warnings. **Tips** provide additional information about PowerPoint 2000 that can help you save time and be more productive. **Notes** offer generally helpful facts that are not specific to PowerPoint 2000. **Warnings** alert you to potential problems that are easy to avoid once you know about them.

There's even more help on the First Steps Web site, where you can **download the student files** necessary in many of these lessons. Use any Web browser to go to **www.dryden.com/infosys/fs2k**, and click "Download Student Files."

After working through the steps, you can test your understanding in the end-of-chapter exercises, questions and problems.

First Steps: PowerPoint 2000 was written by Teresa Adams and Stella Smith, who teach software applications courses at Georgia Perimeter College.

Download student files at www.dryden.com/infosys/fs2k. Click the link "Download Student Files."

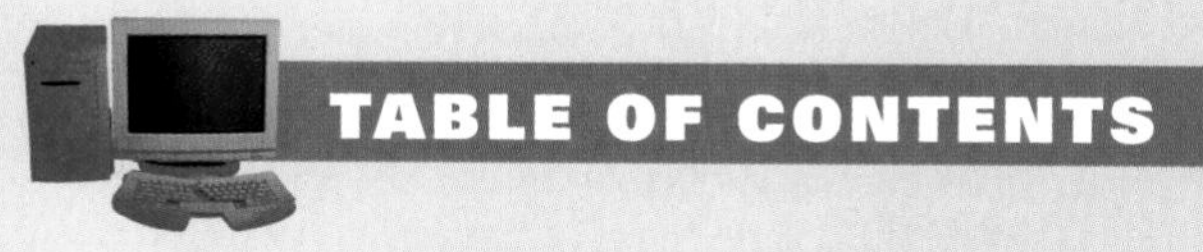
TABLE OF CONTENTS

Getting Started with PowerPoint 2000

OUTLINE

Understanding PowerPoint
Opening an Existing Presentation
Exploring the PowerPoint Interface
Getting Help in PowerPoint
Saving an Existing Presentation
Editing an Existing Slide
Inserting a New Slide
Running the Slide Show
The Views of PowerPoint
Closing a Presentation and Exiting PowerPoint
Strengthening Your Skills
Summary of Functions
Self-Test Problems and Answers

LEARNING OBJECTIVES

After completing this chapter, you will be able to

- Understand the applications of a presentation program
- Start PowerPoint from Windows 95 or 98
- Open an existing PowerPoint presentation
- Explore the PowerPoint window
- Use PowerPoint Help features
- Edit an existing slide
- Insert a new slide
- Work with the PowerPoint views
- Close a presentation and exit PowerPoint

Understanding PowerPoint

PowerPoint is a **presentation graphics program** that allows you to create professional presentations on the computer. You can use PowerPoint to present information for varied situations such as emphasizing the key points in a new marketing plan or training employees how to handle customer complaints.

Instead of displaying your work on pages, as a word processor does, PowerPoint displays your work on the screen as slides. You can view one or many slides at a single time and can print them out in a variety of formats.

PowerPoint provides the tools to engage your audience during a presentation. Visual effects, such as shading and color, add interest to your slides. Bulleted lists, tables, charts, and graphic images allow you to display data in a variety of ways. Techniques incorporating animation and sound can enhance text, images, and, ultimately, your message.

In the step-by-step tutorials for this book, you will use professionally designed backgrounds, page layouts, and wizards to create presentations so that you can focus on content and not be distracted by the design issues. Along with the computer, PowerPoint gives you these options for delivering your presentation:

- Print out **slides** or screens of information on a black-and-white printer.
- Create **overheads** with transparencies printed on a photocopier or color printer.
- Create **35-mm slides** from a file of the presentation.
- Send the presentation electronically or **online** to an interested person.
- Publish the presentation on the **Internet**.

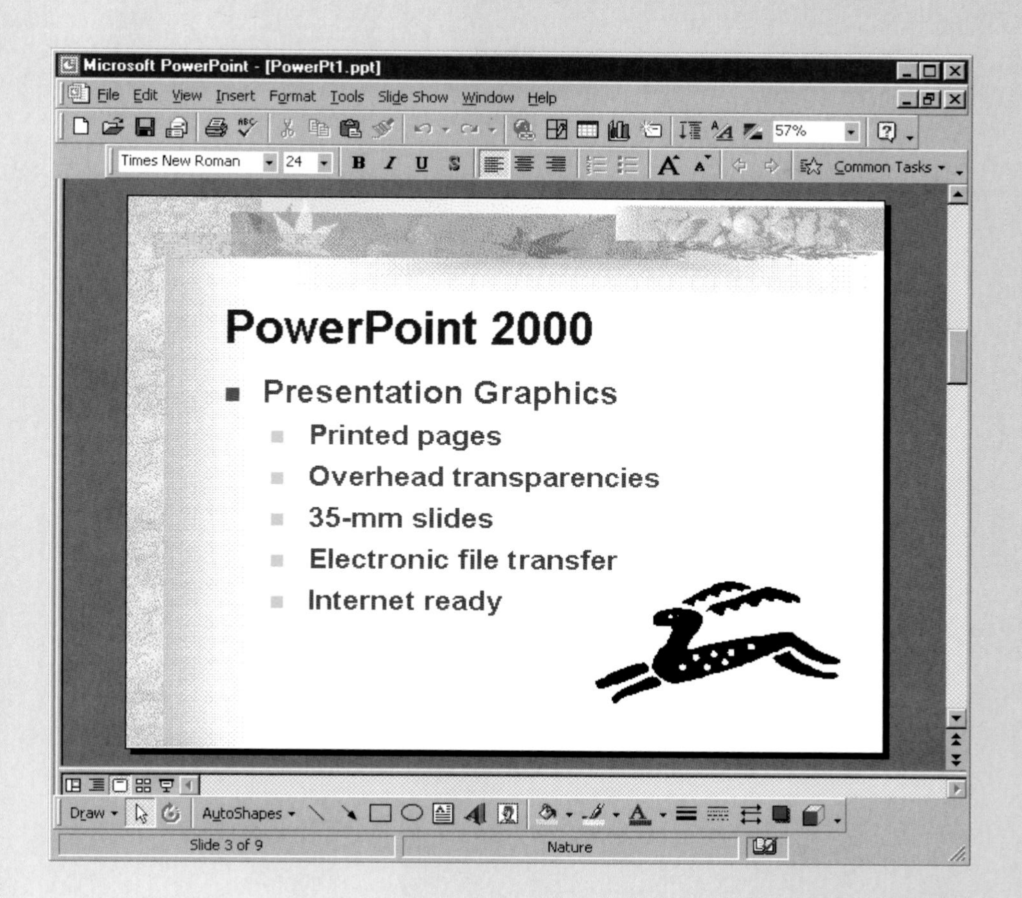
Microsoft PowerPoint - [PowerPt1.ppt]
File Edit View Insert Format Tools Slide Show Window Help
Times New Roman
24
57%
Common Tasks
PowerPoint 2000
Presentation Graphics
Printed pages
Overhead transparencies
35-mm slides
Electronic file transfer
Internet ready
Draw
AutoShapes
Slide 3 of 9
Nature

Opening an Existing Presentation

Before you can create or open a presentation in PowerPoint, you must start the PowerPoint program first. The PowerPoint program can be started from the Windows 95 or 98 task bar. You will start PowerPoint and open an existing presentation in this lesson.

1. Turn on the computer and start Windows.
2. Click the **Start button** Start on the Windows task bar. The Windows Start menu will appear as shown in Figure 1.1.
3. Shift the pointer over the menu choice **Programs**.
4. Locate the program **Microsoft PowerPoint**. Click once on the **Microsoft PowerPoint Icon** Microsoft PowerPoint to launch the application.

(continued on page 6)

FIGURE 1.1
Windows 95 Start Menu

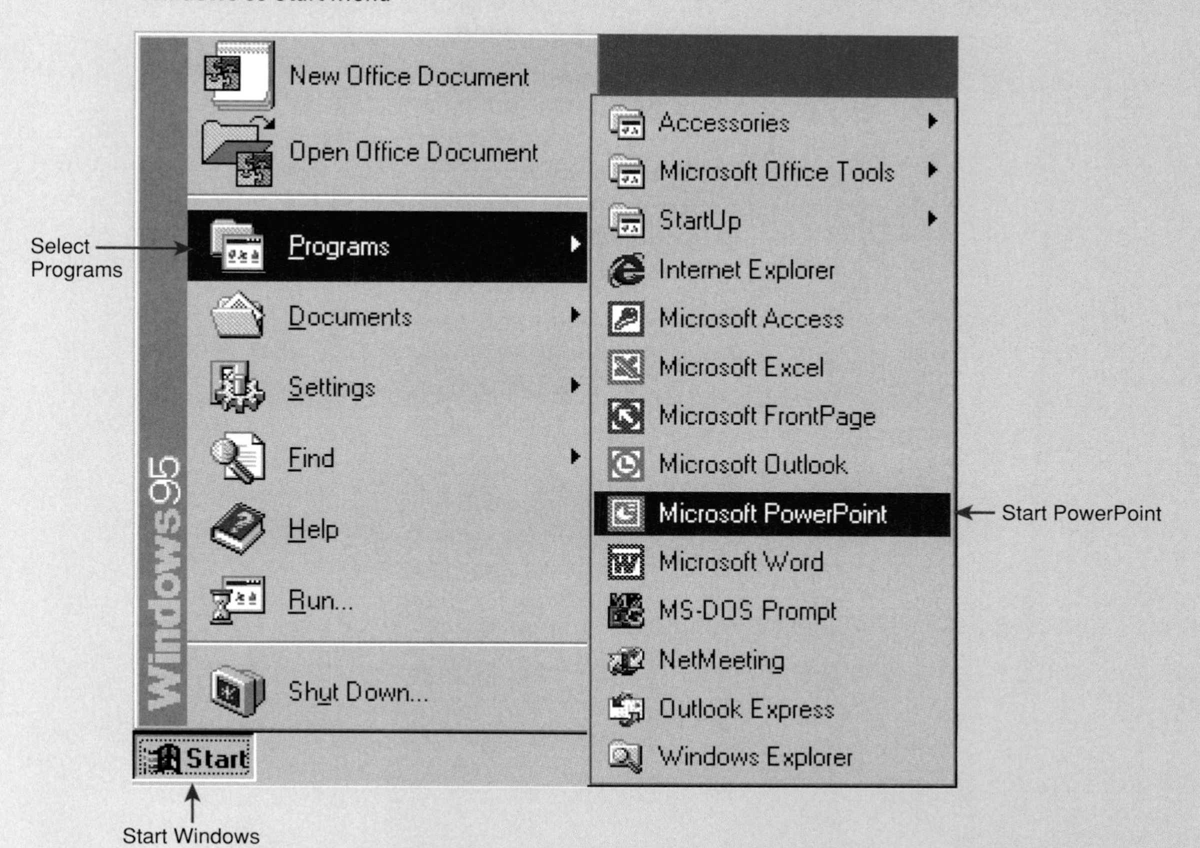

Opening an Existing Presentation (continued)

5. The Microsoft PowerPoint dialog box appears on the screen as shown in Figure 1.2.
6. Click **Open an existing presentation** to view a presentation already created and stored with your student files. (You may download your student files at **www.dryden.com/infosys/fs2k**.)
7. Click **OK** to move to the Open dialog box.
8. In the **Open dialog box**, click the arrow in the **Look-in list box** (Figure 1.3) to select the **A: drive** or wherever your student files are stored.
9. Double-click the file **Instructional Design** to open.

FYI **Using Shortcut Icons**

The PowerPoint program may also be started from a shortcut icon. If your Windows 95 or 98 screen contains a Microsoft PowerPoint program icon or a shortcut icon for Office, you may start PowerPoint by double-clicking on the shortcut.

FIGURE 1.2
Opening an Existing Presentation

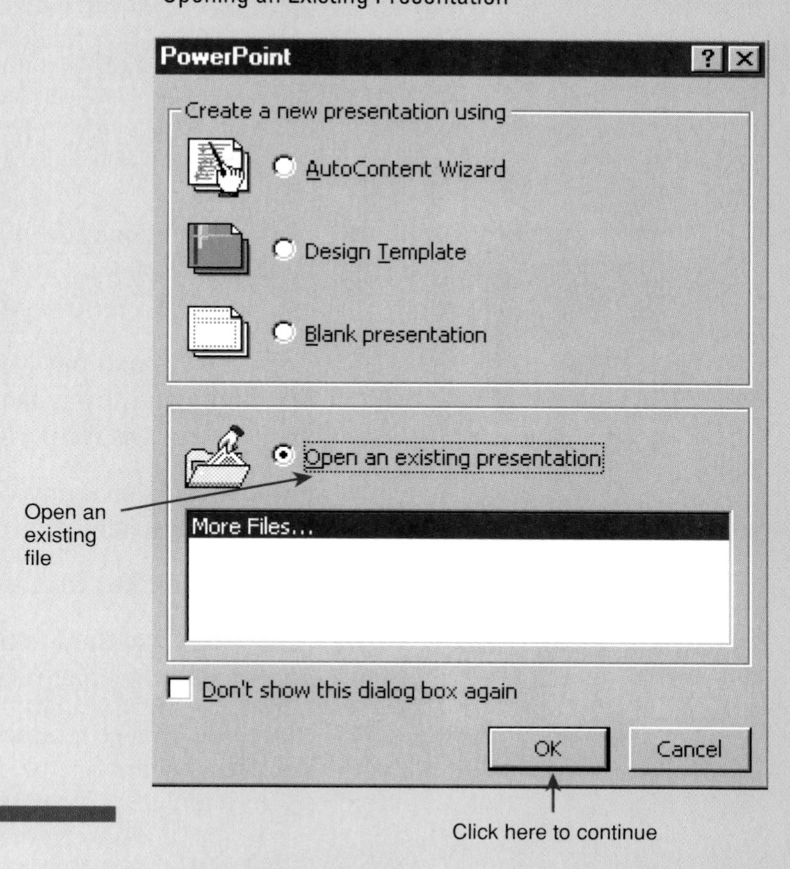

FIGURE 1.3
Opening an Existing Presentation

Select drive where student files are located

Double-click to open file

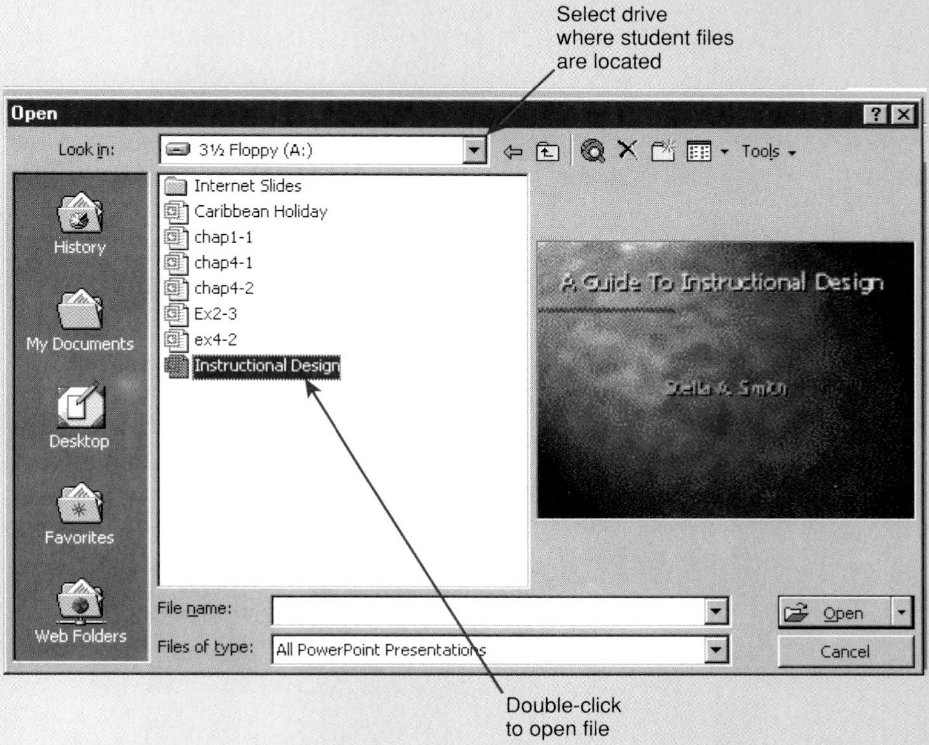

Exploring the PowerPoint Interface

Upon starting PowerPoint, and opening an existing file, the **PowerPoint window** appears on the screen. The PowerPoint window contains a menu and toolbars with buttons to help you create presentations. The following steps will assist you in understanding the PowerPoint interface.

1. If all the toolbars do not appear as shown in Figure 1.4, select **View** in the menu. Click at a specific toolbar to select. If you decide to close a toolbar, simply reclick to deselect.
2. Locate the **menu bar** as shown in Figure 1.4. Click once on the **File** command to invoke the File menu. The File menu contains menu selections for performing various file operations on a slide.
3. Point to the remaining commands on the menu bar and examine the available menu options for each command.
4. Press the **Esc key** to close the menu bar.
5. Locate the **Standard toolbar** as shown in Figure 1.4. This toolbar contains buttons that relate to tasks you are most likely to do.
6. Place the mouse pointer on each **tool** of the toolbar until the **ToolTip** appears on the screen. The ToolTip helps identify what the tool does.

(continued on page 10)

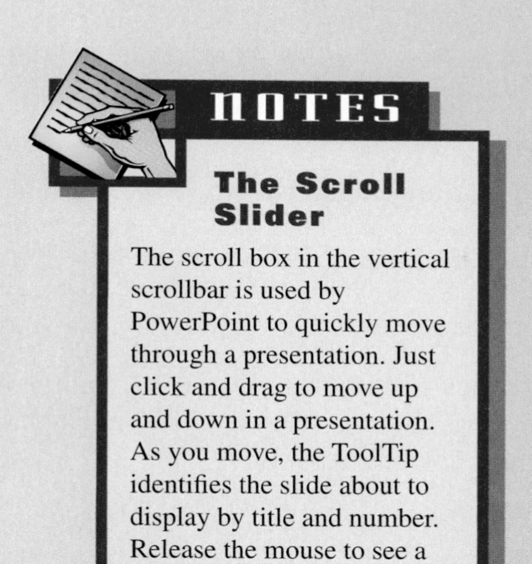

NOTES

The Scroll Slider

The scroll box in the vertical scrollbar is used by PowerPoint to quickly move through a presentation. Just click and drag to move up and down in a presentation. As you move, the ToolTip identifies the slide about to display by title and number. Release the mouse to see a specific slide.

FIGURE 1.4
Microsoft PowerPoint Window

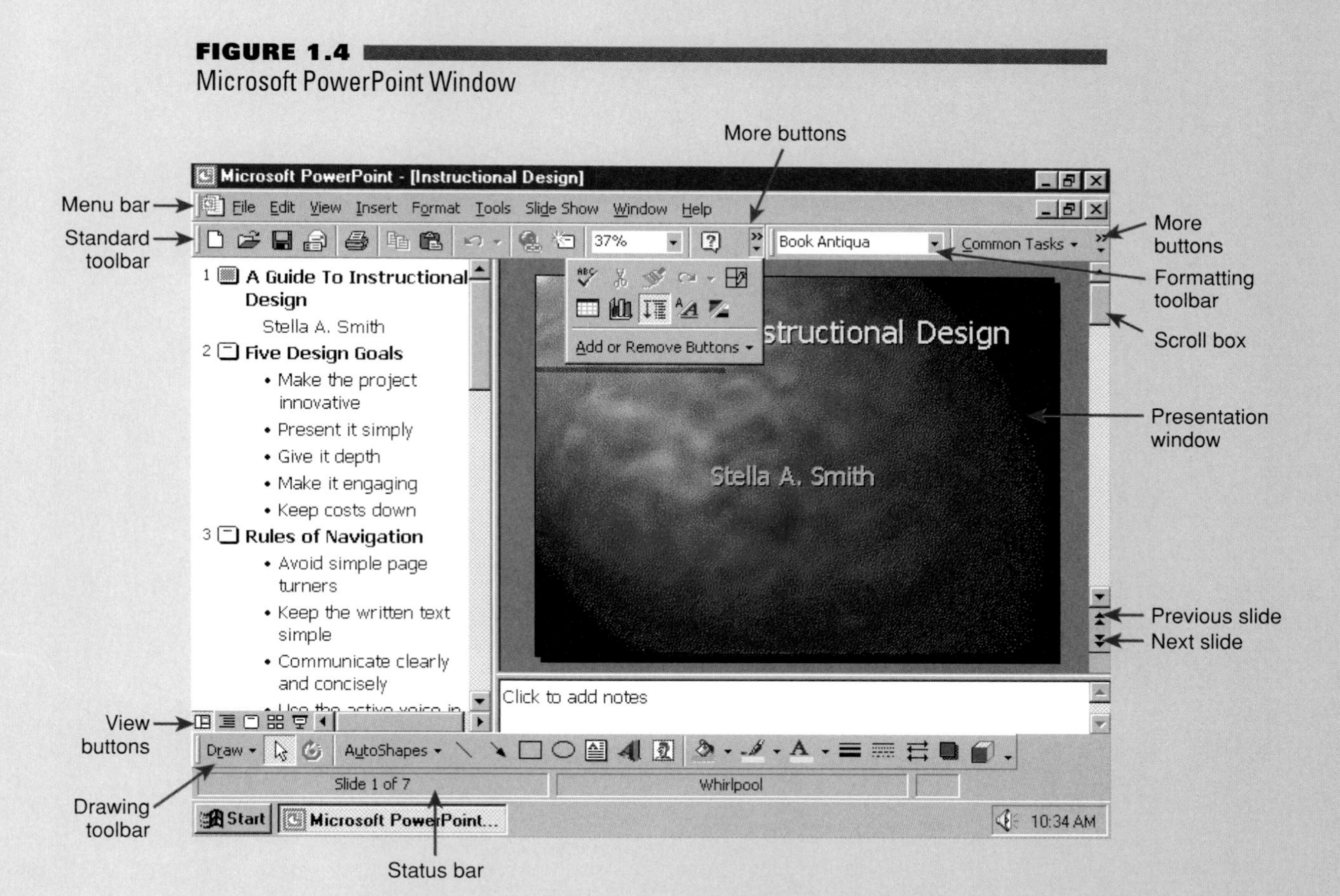

Exploring the PowerPoint Interface (continued)

7. Click **More Buttons** to view additional buttons.
8. Repeat Step 6 for the **Formatting toolbar** (Figure 1.5), containing buttons that change text appearance, and the **Drawing toolbar** (Figure 1.6), containing tools for drawing and creating shapes.
9. A series of buttons at the bottom left corner of the window (Figure 1.7) enables you to change views. You are currently in **Normal View**.
10. Click the **Next Slide** button on the vertical scrollbar at the right side of the screen to view the remaining slides.
11. Click the **Previous Slide** button until you return to the first slide.

FIGURE 1.5
Formatting Toolbar

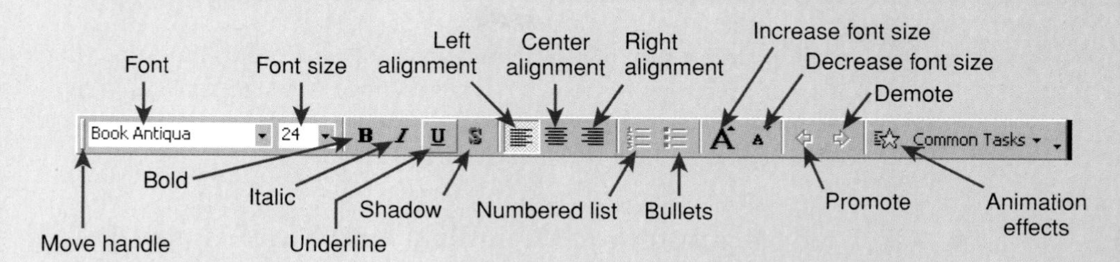

FIGURE 1.6
Drawing Toolbar

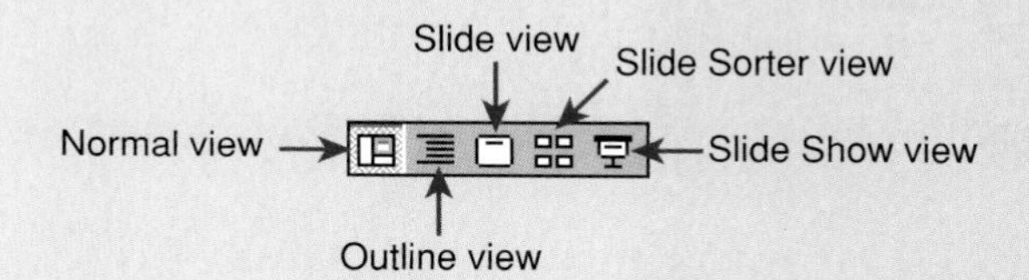

TIP

Floaters and Dockers

A toolbar that appears at the top or around the edges of a window is docked. When it appears elsewhere on the screen, it is a floating toolbar. The Standard and Formatting toolbars are docked side by side. All toolbars can be moved to another location by clicking and dragging on the move handle. Do you want to see what toolbars are available? Simply right-click on a blank space in a toolbar and a list of toolbars will display.

FIGURE 1.7
PowerPoint's Five Views

Getting Help in PowerPoint

PowerPoint provides help in a variety of ways. These include ToolTips, which you worked with in the previous lesson, the Office Assistant, and Help in the menu. You may also use the Office Assistant, an animated message box that allows you to search for help on any task or command.

1. Click the Microsoft PowerPoint **Help button** in the standard toolbar.
2. The **Office Assistant** will display on the screen as shown in Figure 1.8.
3. Locate the **Query text box** and type in the topic **What is a shadow?**
4. Click the **Search button** to see the topics related to shadowing. Select **Add a shadow to text**.
5. Click the **Show button**. Click on the **Index tab** to bring it to the front.
6. Type **shadow** as shown in Figure 1.9. Click the **Search button** to view related topics.
7. Click the **Close button** to exit the index list.
8. Select **Help** in the Menu toolbar.
9. Select **What's This?** Your cursor assumes the shape of a question mark.
10. Move your mouse to the **Shadow button**. You may need to click More Buttons to find the Shadow button. Click it to read about the shadow function. Click outside of the message to close.

FIGURE 1.8
Office Assistant Window

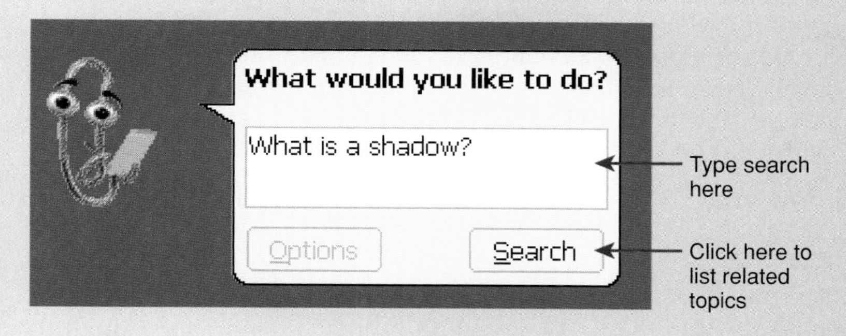

TIP

Meeting the Office Assistant

The Office Assistant icon may appear automatically on the screen upon starting your application. If you see a light bulb, clicking on it will bring a tip to the screen related to your current task. Many users choose to leave the Office Assistant on the screen while working in the application. You may also choose to close it by right-clicking on the Office Assistant and selecting Hide the Office Assistant.

FIGURE 1.9
Contents and Index in Help

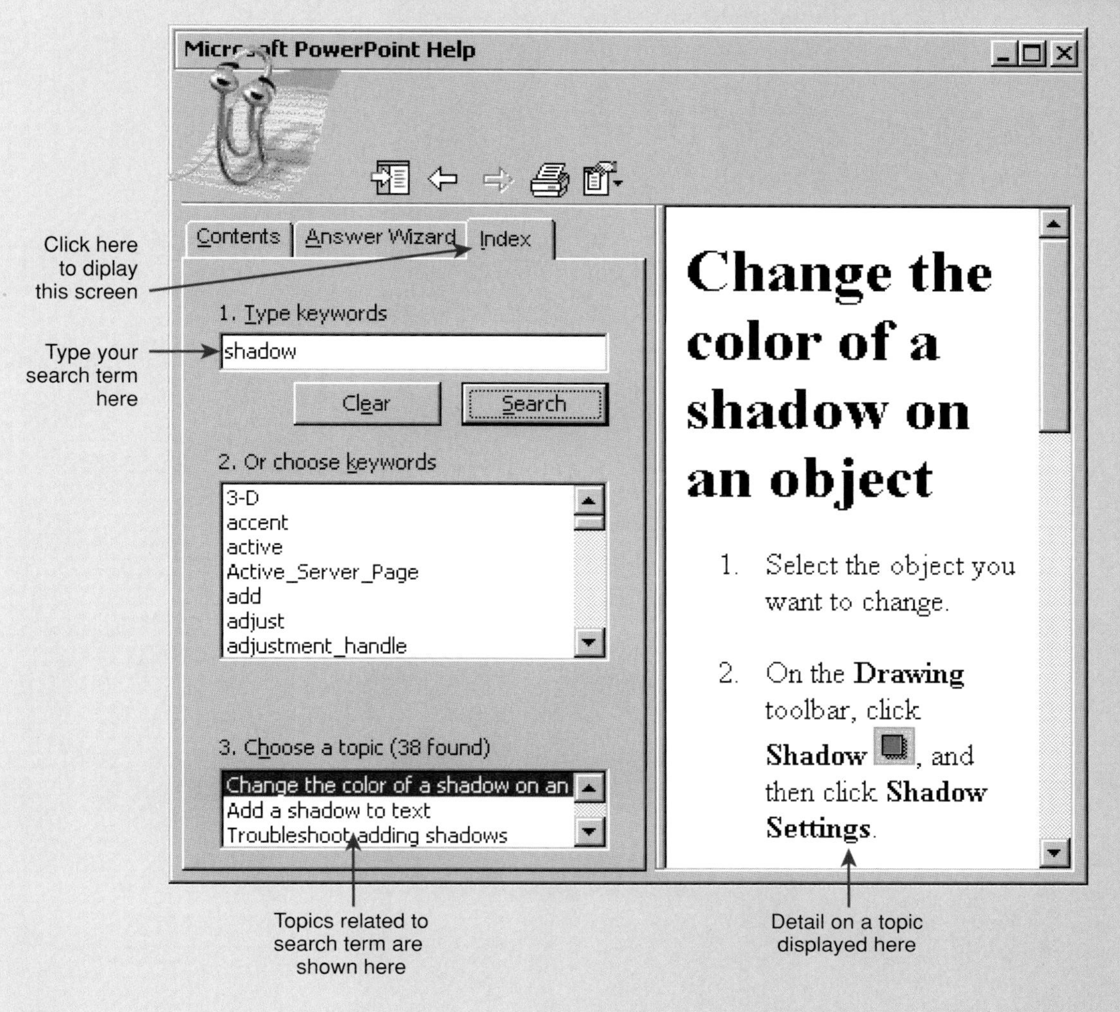

Saving an Existing Presentation

You should be in the PowerPoint presentation titled Instructional Design. If you are not, open PowerPoint and select that file. You will rename the file so that the original remains unchanged and save the file into a file folder.

1. Pull down the **File** menu. Click **Save As** to display the File Save dialog box as shown in Figure 1.10.
2. Enter **Revised Instructional Design** as the new name of this presentation. (A file name may contain up to 255 characters, including spaces.)
3. The default folder is My Documents. Let's change the folder name to **PowerPoint Slides**.
4. Click the **Create New Folder** button in the Save As window to create a new folder for your first document.
5. Type in **PowerPoint Slides** as the name of your new folder as shown in Figure 1.11.

(continued on page 16)

FIGURE 1.10
Save As Dialog Box

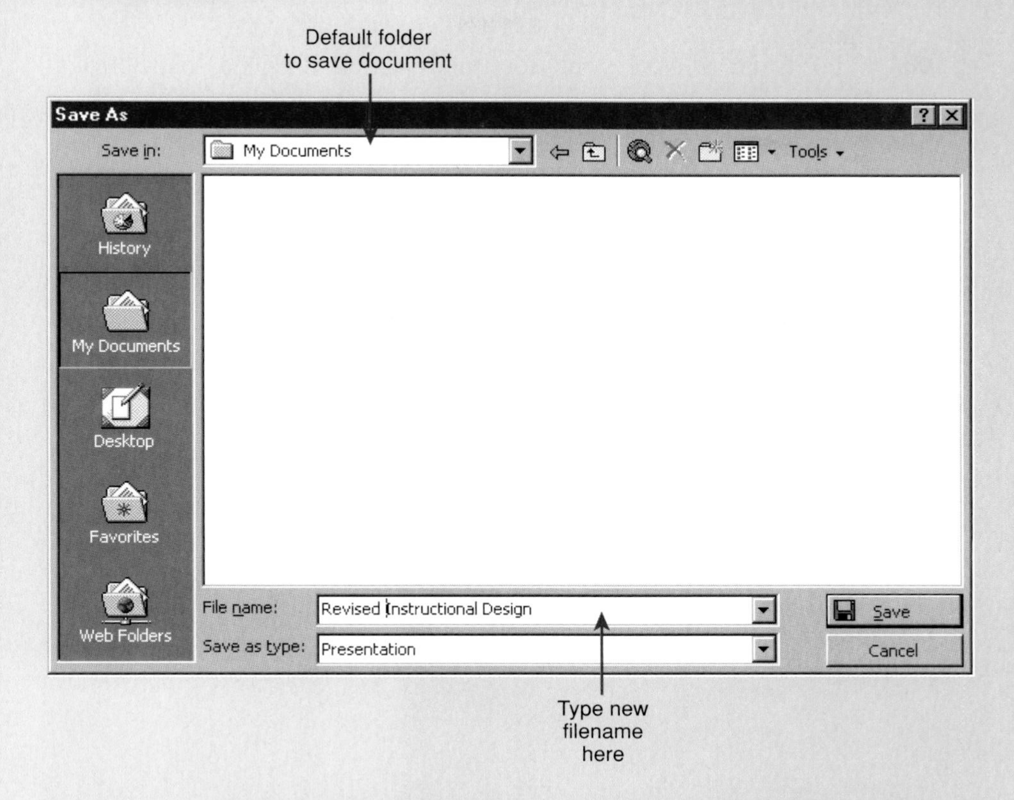

FIGURE 1.11
New Folder

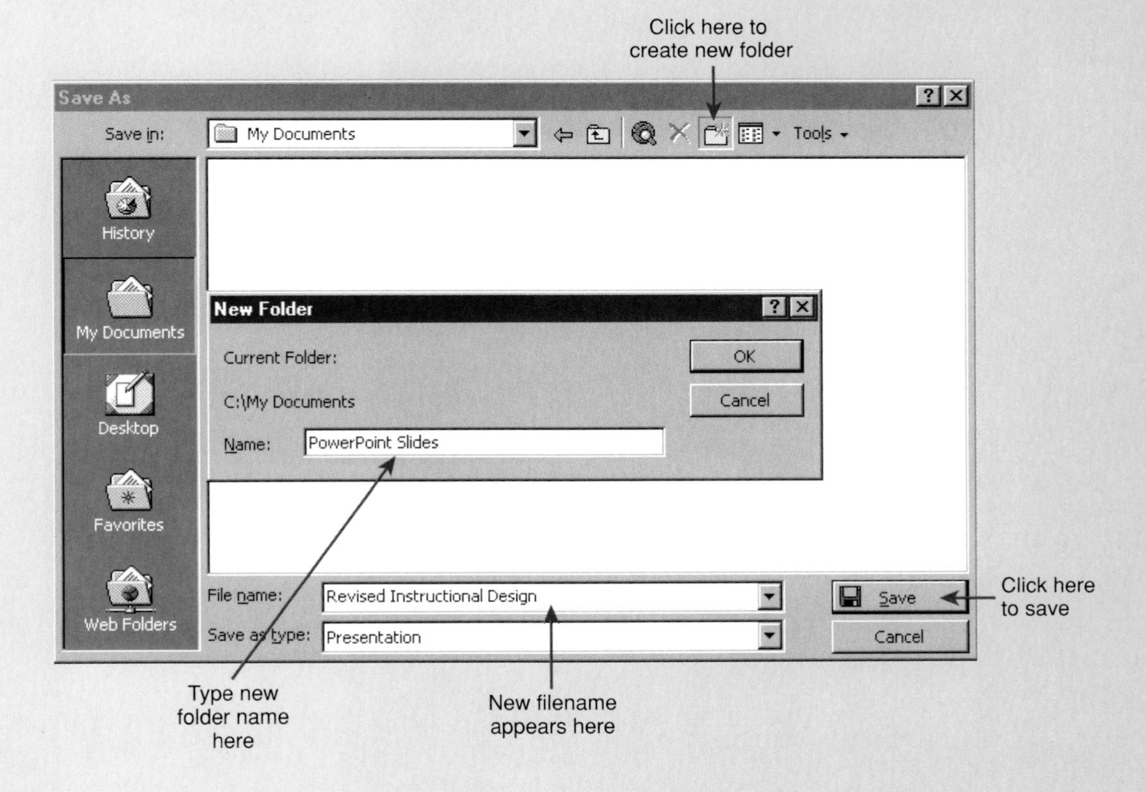

Saving an Existing Presentation (continued)

6. Click **Save** to save your document called Revised Instructional Design into the folder called PowerPoint Slides as shown in Figure 1.12.

FIGURE 1.12
Document Saved with a New Name

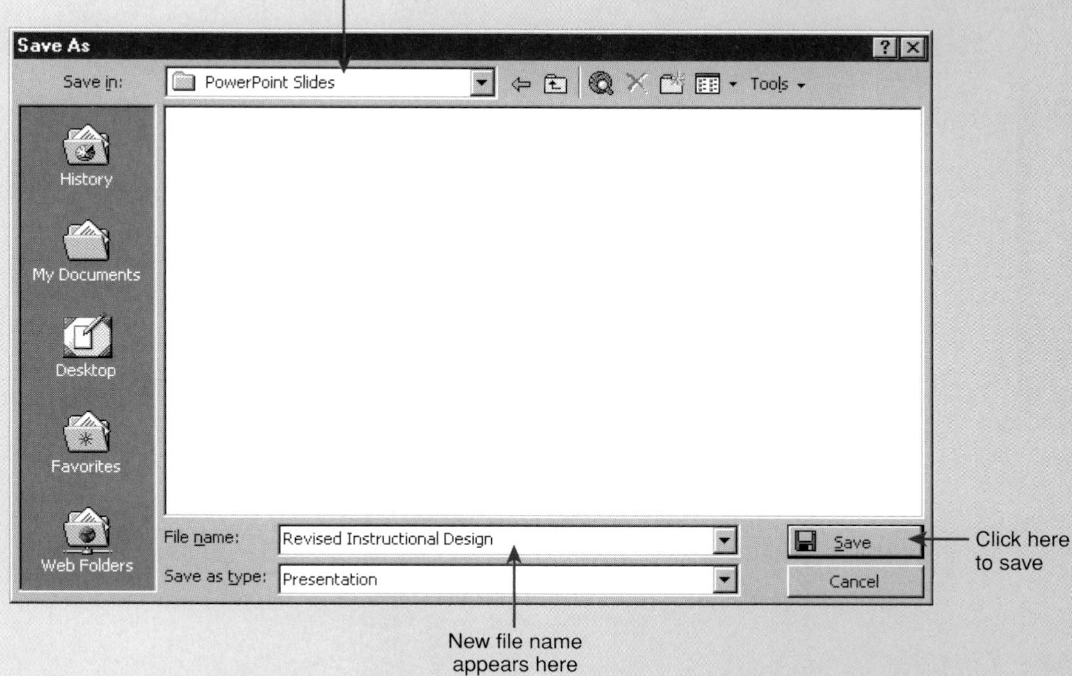

NOTES

Saving to Your Floppy Disk

1. Insert a formatted 3½" floppy disk into the diskette drive. (You may have a student disk that contains all your student files. If not, download them from www.dryden.com/infosys/fs2k/.)
2. Click File on the menu bar.
3. Move the pointer down to Save As and click once to open the Save As dialog box.
4. Click Save In to open a list of drives available to you.
5. Click the 3½" floppy A:
6. Type the appropriate file name in the File name text box.
7. Click Save in the dialog box to save your file.

Editing an Existing Slide

You should be in the file Revised Instructional Design. If you have exited PowerPoint, restart the program and open this file to continue with the tutorials. In this lesson, you will learn how to edit a slide in an existing presentation.

1. You should be in Normal View. Click on **Slide View** so that the slide occupies most of the screen.
2. Click anywhere on the author's name to select it for editing. You should see a box appear around the name as shown in Figure 1.13.
3. Move your flashing insertion point to the beginning of the author's name and drag it across. The name should be highlighted as shown in Figure 1.13.
4. Type in **your name** as a replacement. Your name automatically replaces the selected text.
5. Click outside the selected area to **deselect** it. Refer to Figure 1.14 to view the finished slide.

FIGURE 1.13
Selected Text

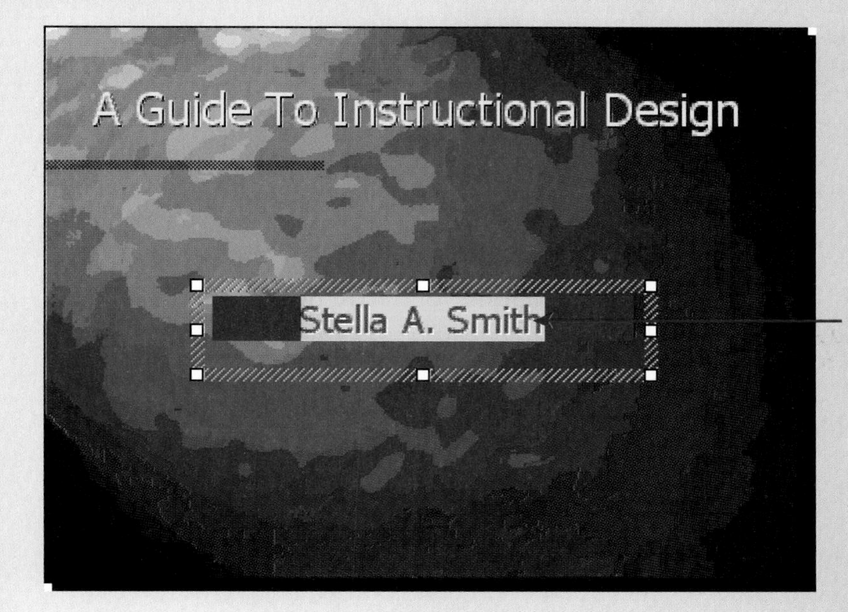

Click anywhere in the name to select this object for editing

NOTES

Select Then Edit

Slides are made up of objects. These objects may be text, graphics, or charts. Once an object is selected, you can change its position, size, and appearance. If a block of text is selected, you can click the boldface or italics button to change its appearance. Similarly, once selected, a block of text can be deleted by pressing the Del key. The quickest way to select a block of text is to click and drag the insertion point across the text.

FIGURE 1.14
Edited Slide

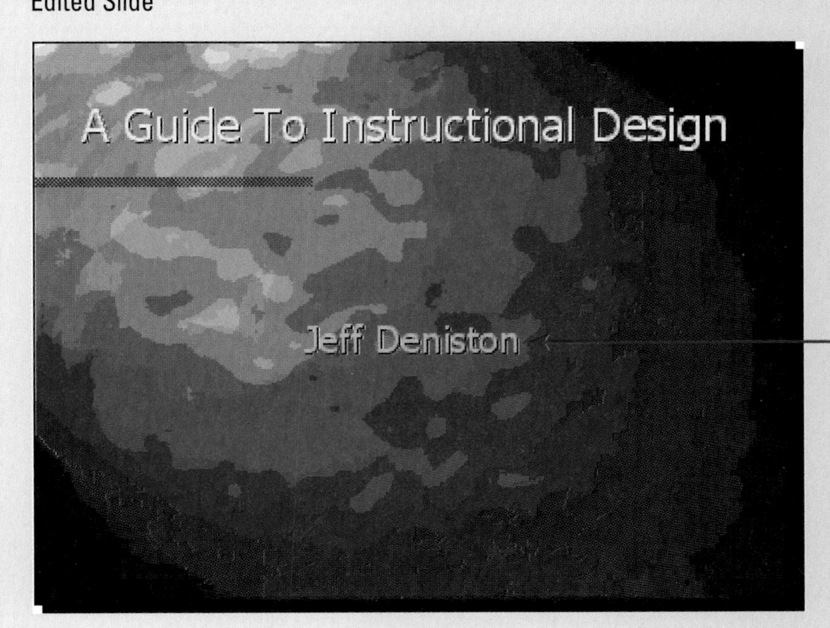

Your name will appear here

Inserting a New Slide

When editing a presentation, you may decide to add slides. Inserting a new slide while you are in Slide View displays the Auto Layout feature. Auto Layout provides many different options for displaying your information. In this lesson, you will add a slide and select a predefined layout from the New Slide dialog box.

1. Go to **Slide 6** by clicking and dragging the scroll box. Notice the slide title and number appear as you move down the scroll bar as shown in Figure 1.15.
2. Click **Insert** on the menu and click **New Slide** (or click the New Slide button) .
3. The New Slide dialog box appears with options for predefined layouts. Double-click to select the option shown in Figure 1.16. (This indicates a heading and bulleted items.)

(continued on page 22)

FIGURE 1.15
Scroll Box as Navigator

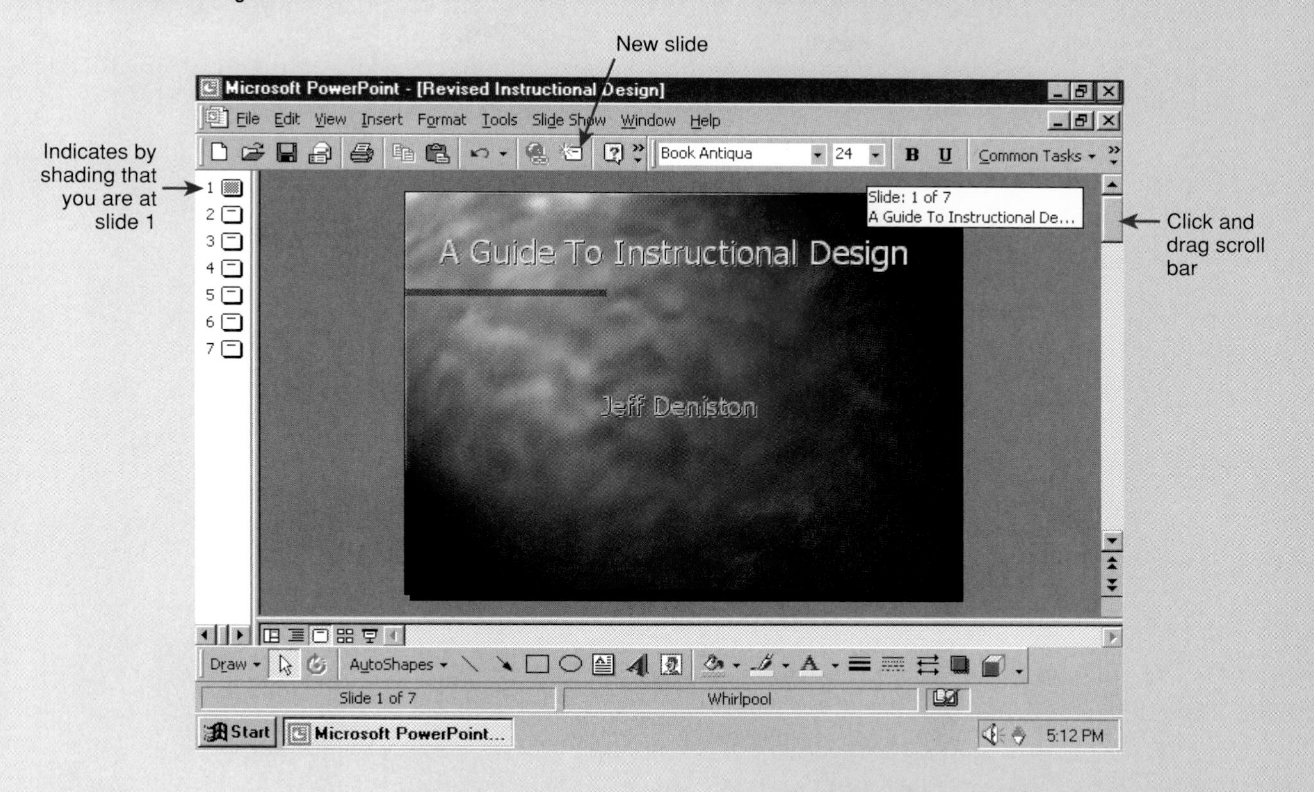

FIGURE 1.16
New Slide Dialog Box

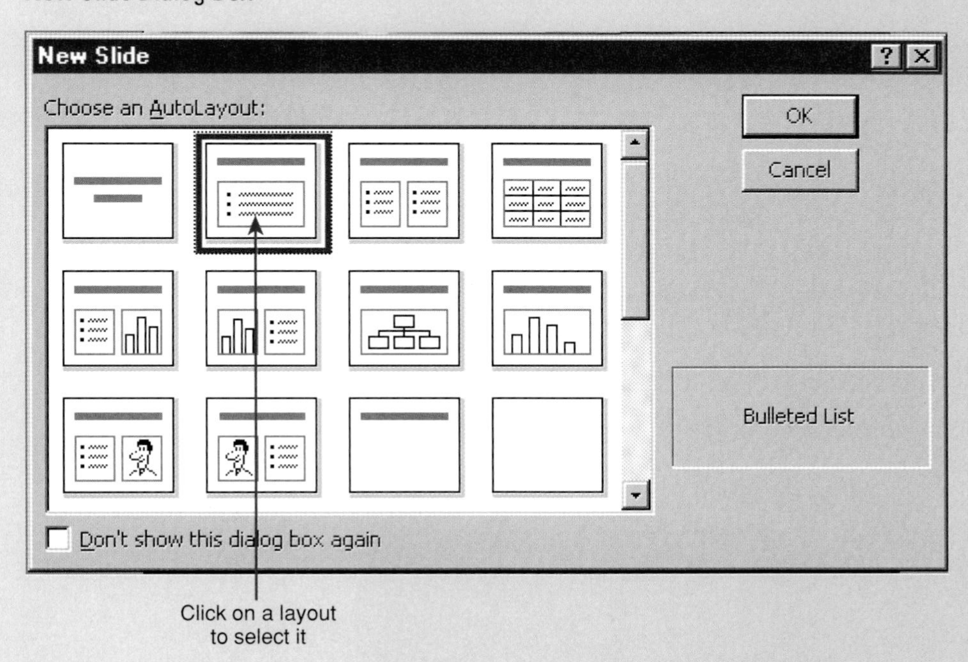

Inserting a New Slide (continued)

4. The **new slide** appears with placeholders directing you to the areas to edit as shown in Figure 1.17.

5. Click in the **title area** and type **Brainstorming** as shown in Figure 1.18.

(continued on page 24)

FIGURE 1.17
New Slide

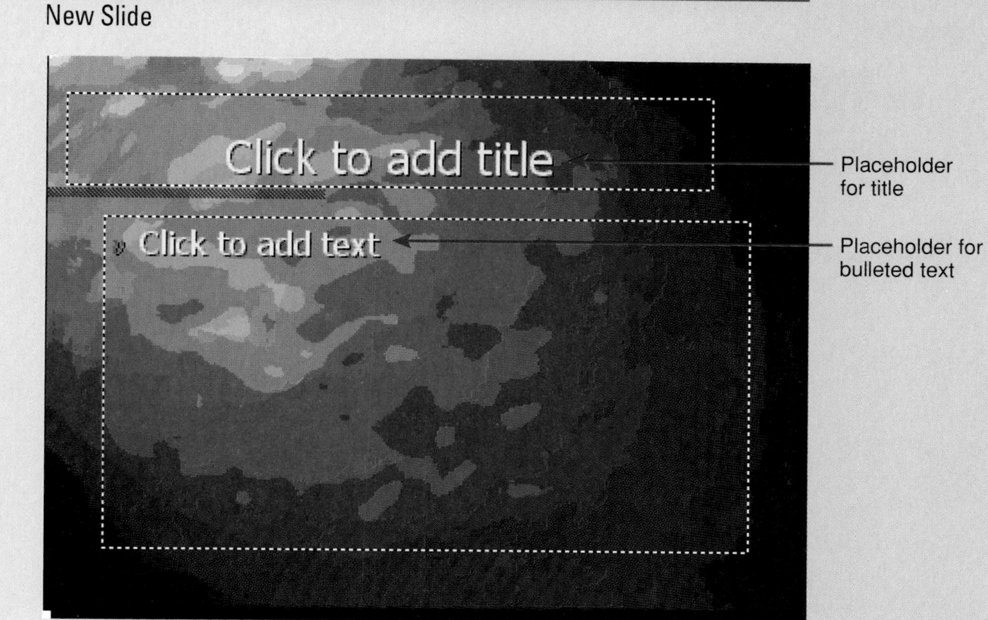

FIGURE 1.18
Slide with Title

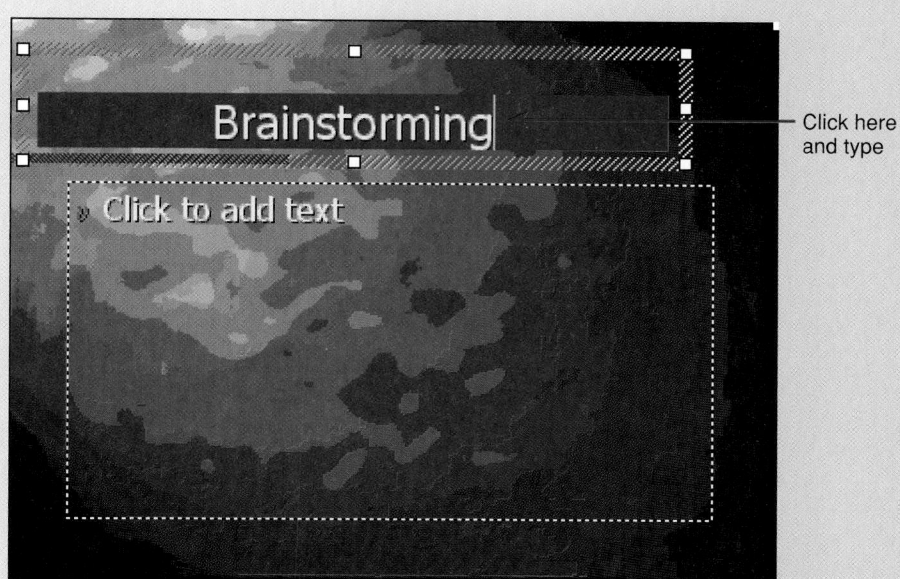

Inserting a New Slide (continued)

6. Click in the **text area** and **type** the text as shown in Figure 1.19.
7. Click outside the text area to remove the editing box. Compare your screen to Figure 1.20.
8. **Save** your work .

FYI PowerPoint's **AutoLayout** feature provides 24 layouts to assist you in arranging the objects in your slides in a visually appealing way. **Placeholders** for text and other objects appear on the AutoLayout automatically. All placeholders, such as bulleted lists, clip art, charts, tables, and organization charts, can be moved around the screen. If you decide to change a layout, the information on the slide will remain unchanged.

FIGURE 1.19
Text Inserted in Text Box

Brainstorming
Writers, designers and directors all working together to generate and record ideas.
Click here and type

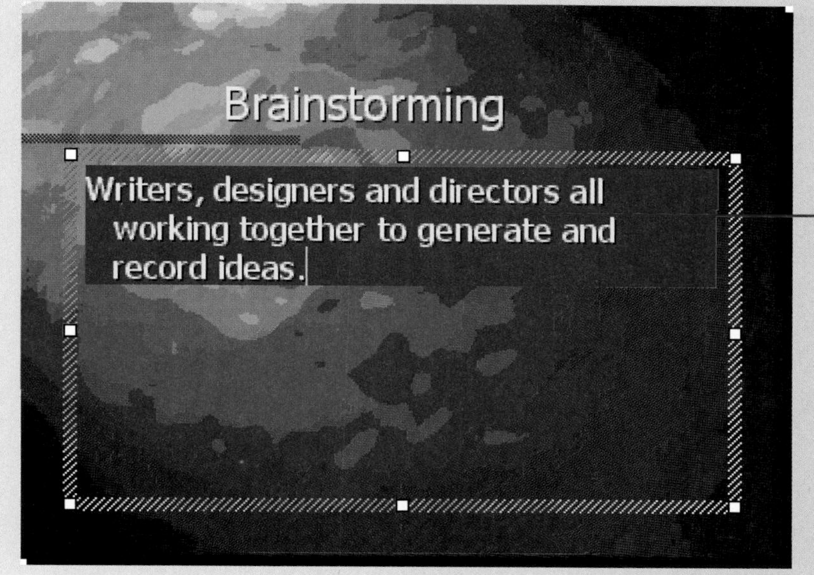

FIGURE 1.20
The New Slide

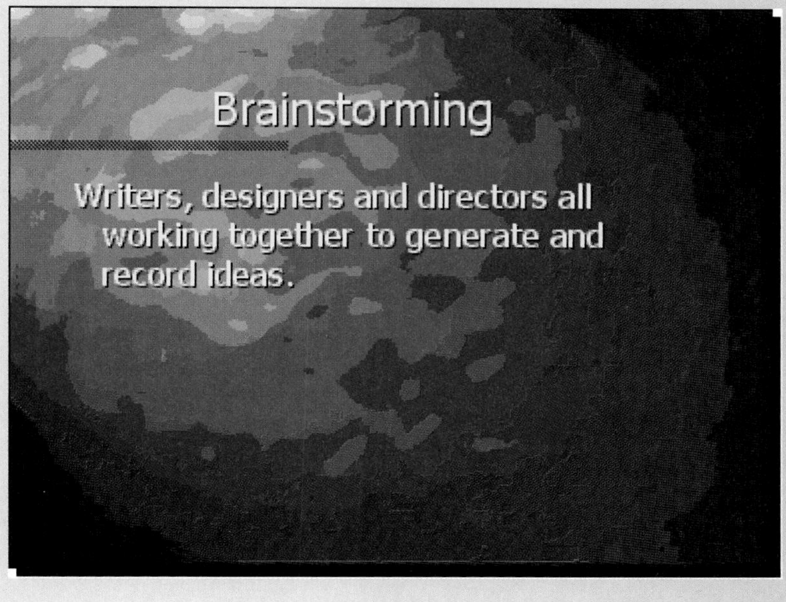

Brainstorming
Writers, designers and directors all working together to generate and record ideas.

Running the Slide Show

You are now ready to view the presentation as a slide show. You will set up the presentation to run manually and see the presentation as it will appear on the computer screen.

1. Move to **slide 1** of your presentation by clicking the **Previous Slide button** or moving the scroll box on the vertical scroll bar.
2. Click the **Slide Show** button at the bottom left of your screen on the View toolbar.
3. **Advance** through each slide manually by clicking the mouse button or pressing the Enter key on your keyboard.
4. Move the mouse to display the **triangle** in a box at the bottom left corner of each slide in the slide show (Figure 1.21). Click the button to view the navigation commands on the pop-up menu.
5. Click outside the menu to close it.
6. Continue clicking at each slide or pressing Enter until you finish the show.

FIGURE 1.21
Controlling the Slide Show

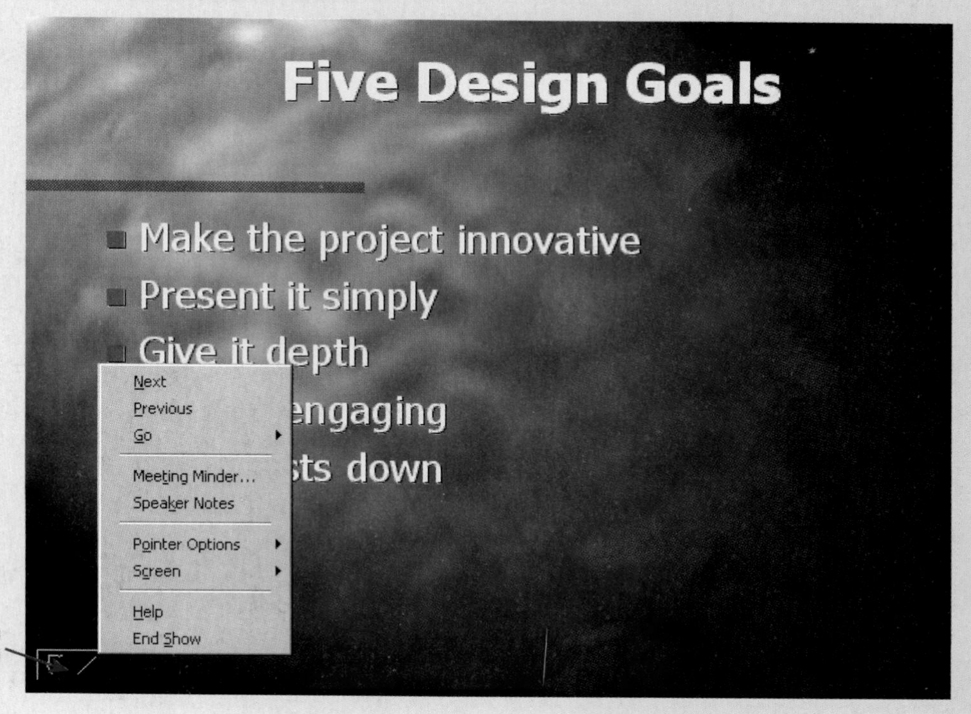

NOTES

Slide Show View Shortcuts

PowerPoint provides keyboard shortcuts to speed up navigation in a slide show. They are listed below.

Action	Result
Mouse click	Go to the next slide
Right-mouse click	Go to the previous slide
Press Enter	Go to the next slide
Press Home	Go to the first slide in the show
Press End	Go to the last slide in the show
Press PgUp	Go to the previous slide
Press PgDn	Go to the next slide
Press a slide number, and then press Enter	Go to the slide number you specified

TIP

Let's Start the Show!

Another way to start a slide show is to select View, Slide Show in the menu or Slide Show, View Show. To quit a show at any time, press the Esc key.

WARNING

Patience!

The template guiding this presentation has built-in animation that moves a line across the top left of the screen. Give it a chance to display. Pressing the Enter key or clicking a mouse button will not move you to the next screen until the current screen, with all its built-in features, is fully displayed.

The Views of PowerPoint

PowerPoint provides five different views to assist you during the development of your slide presentation: Normal, Slide, Outline, Slide Sorter, and Slide Show. Each view is helpful for specific tasks. For instance, Outline view shows the overall organization of a presentation, while Slide Sorter enables you to rearrange slides. You have already accessed the Slide and Slide Show views. You will now examine the remaining views in the following steps.

1. If you are not in the file **Revised Instructional Design**, open the file.
2. Click the **Outline view button** in the bottom left-hand corner of the PowerPoint window. Refer to Figure 1.22 for the features available in Outline view.

(continued on page 30)

FIGURE 1.22
Outline View

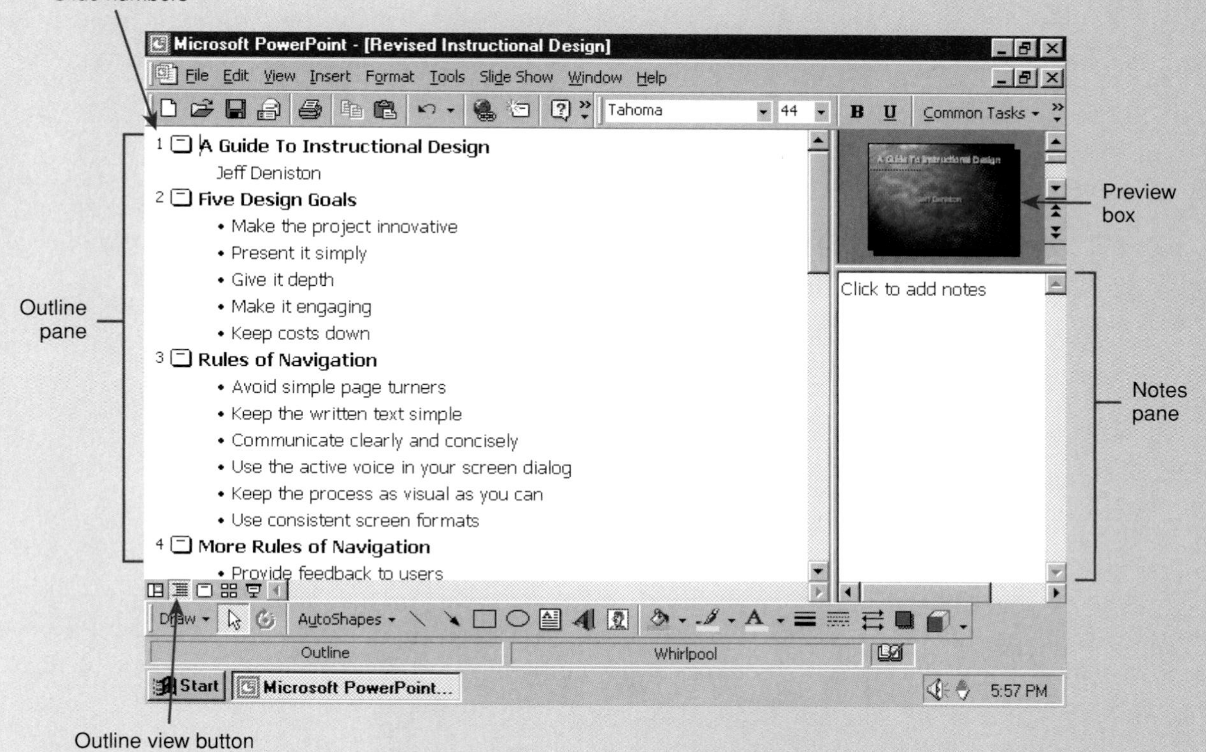

The Views of PowerPoint (continued)

3. Scroll down to slide number 7 titled **Brainstorming** and click your flashing insertion point at the word *directors*. Delete and replace with **subject matter experts** (Figure 1.23).
4. Click the **Slide Sorter view** button .
5. Click slide number 7 to select it. You'll see a solid border around the slide indicating it has been selected.
6. Place your pointer on the slide, then click and drag it on top of slide number 8. (Notice your pointer changes shape.)
7. Look at Figure 1.24 to see the new order of the slides. The Brainstorming slide is now the last slide in the show.

(continued on page 32)

FIGURE 1.23
Edited Slide in Outline View

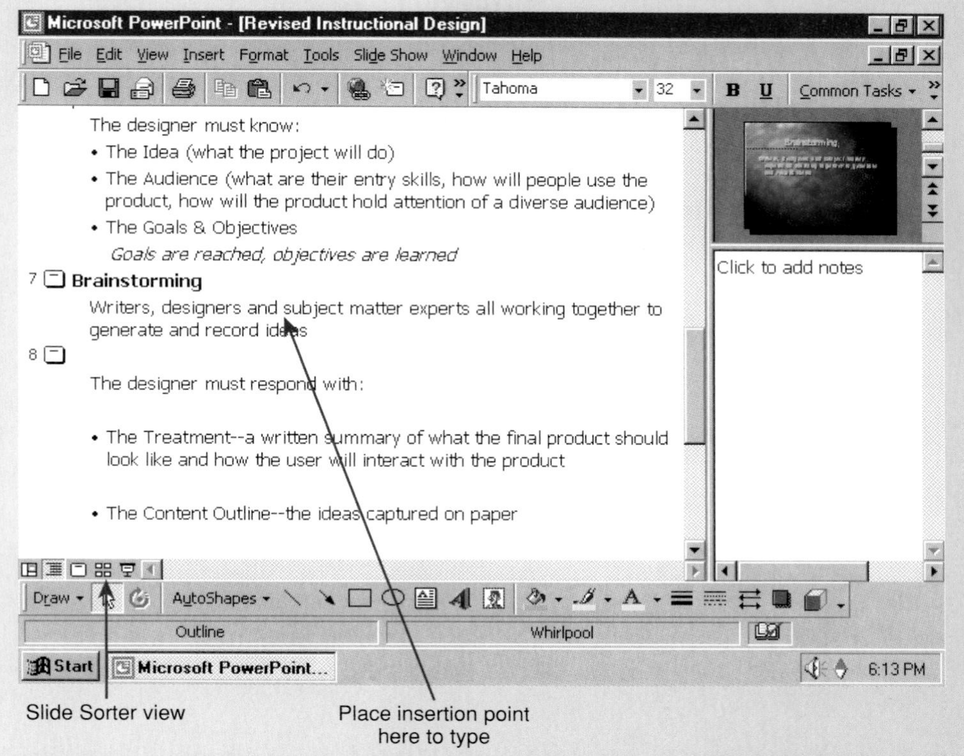

FIGURE 1.24
Slide Sorter View

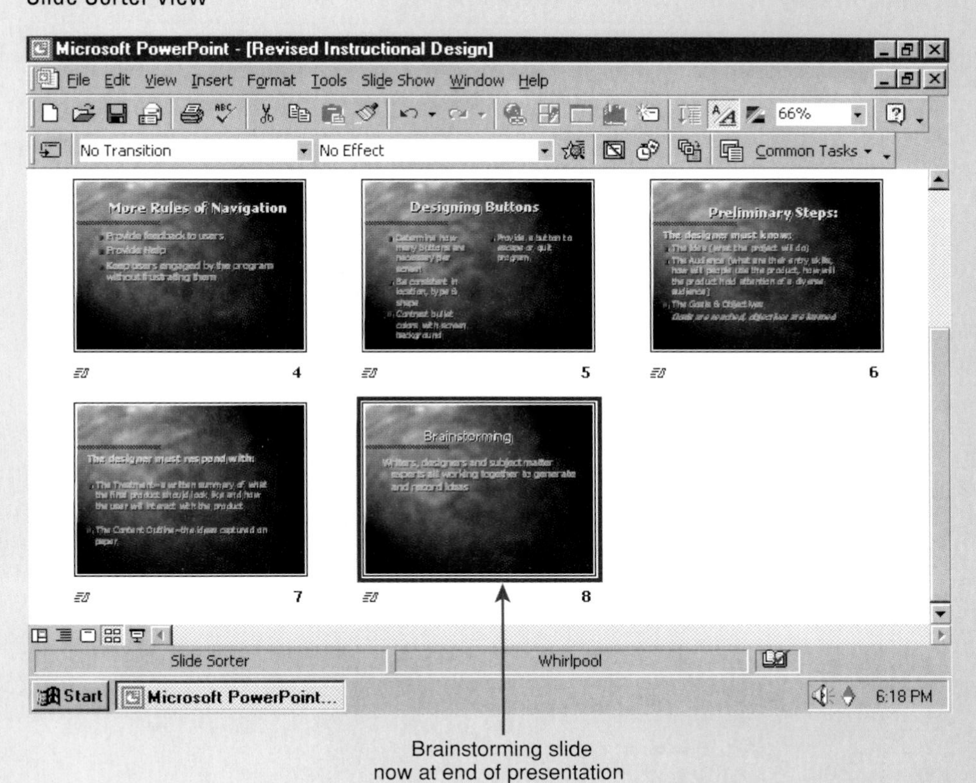

TIP

Slide Mini-Window

To see a miniature of a slide, select View in the menu, click Slide Miniature. The Slide Miniature appears automatically when you change slides to a black-and-white view, when you zoom so that your slide is not appearing, or when you are in title master or slide master view.

The Views of PowerPoint (continued)

8. Click the **Outline view button** . Click in the Notes pane and type: Demonstration of brainstorming using case study (Figure 1.25).

9. Click the **Slide view button** to return to viewing a single slide.

FIGURE 1.25
Notes Pane

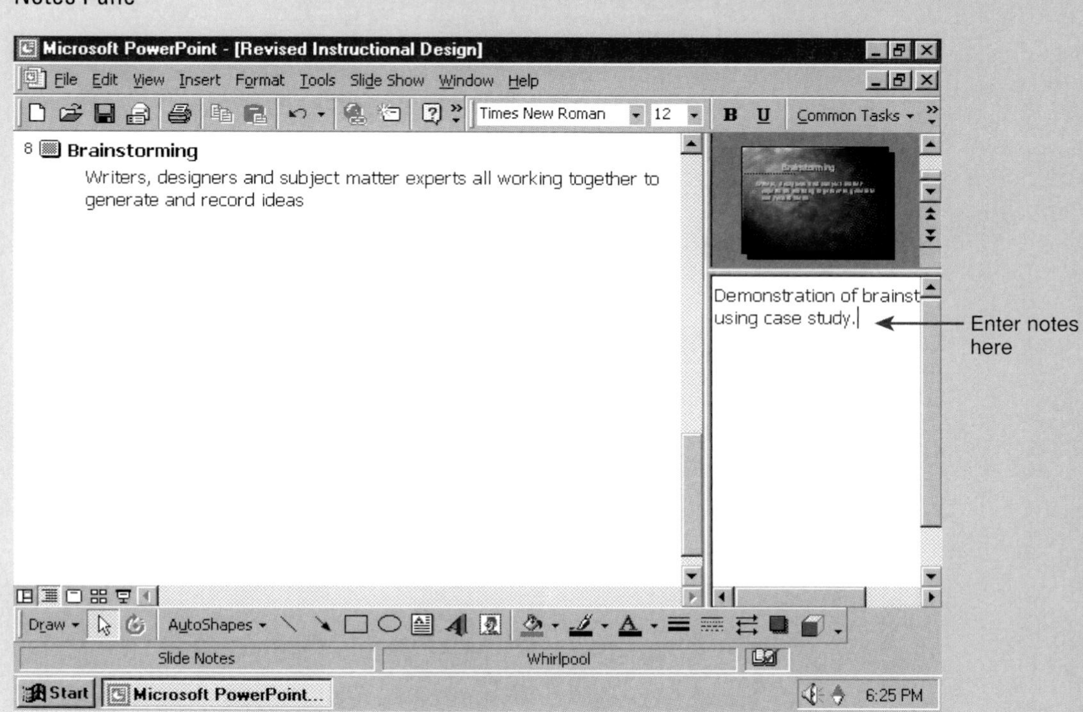

Closing a Presentation and Exiting PowerPoint

When you are finished using a PowerPoint file, you should close the file.

1. Click the **File** command on the menu bar, and then click **Close**, as shown in Figure 1.26.

   OR

   Click the **Close button** ☒ on the file window.

2. Click **Yes** to save your changes.

3. To exit PowerPoint, click the **File** command on the menu bar, and then click **Exit**.

   OR

   Click the **Close button** ☒ on the PowerPoint window.

FIGURE 1.26
File Menu

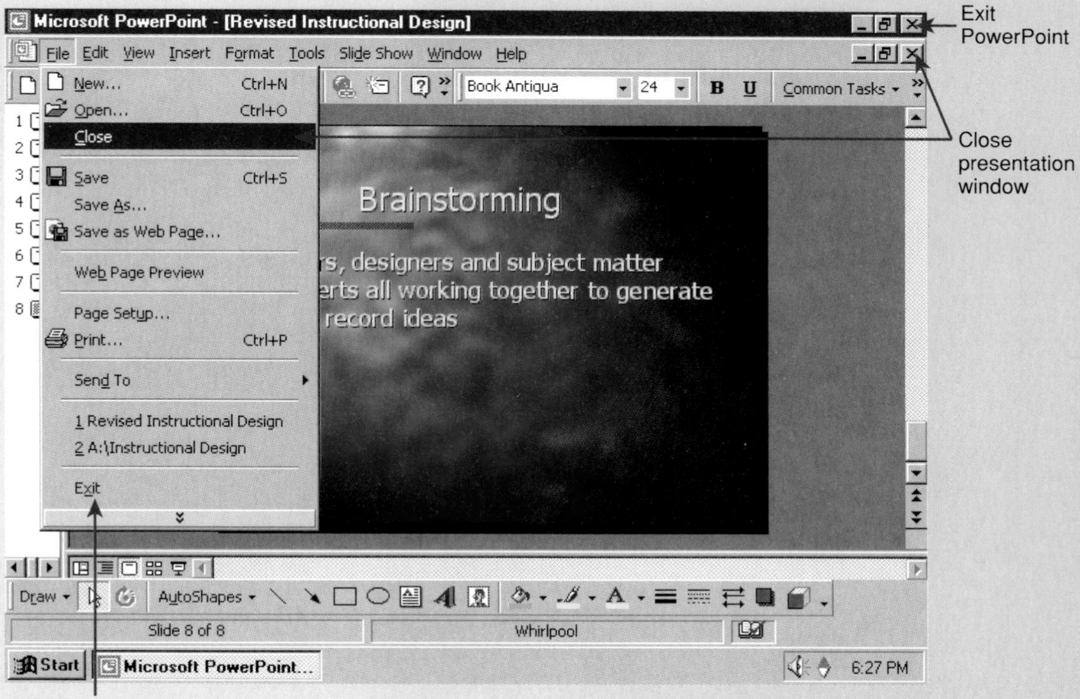

STRENGTHENING YOUR SKILLS

1. Refer to the figure below for a view of a presentation and answer the following questions:

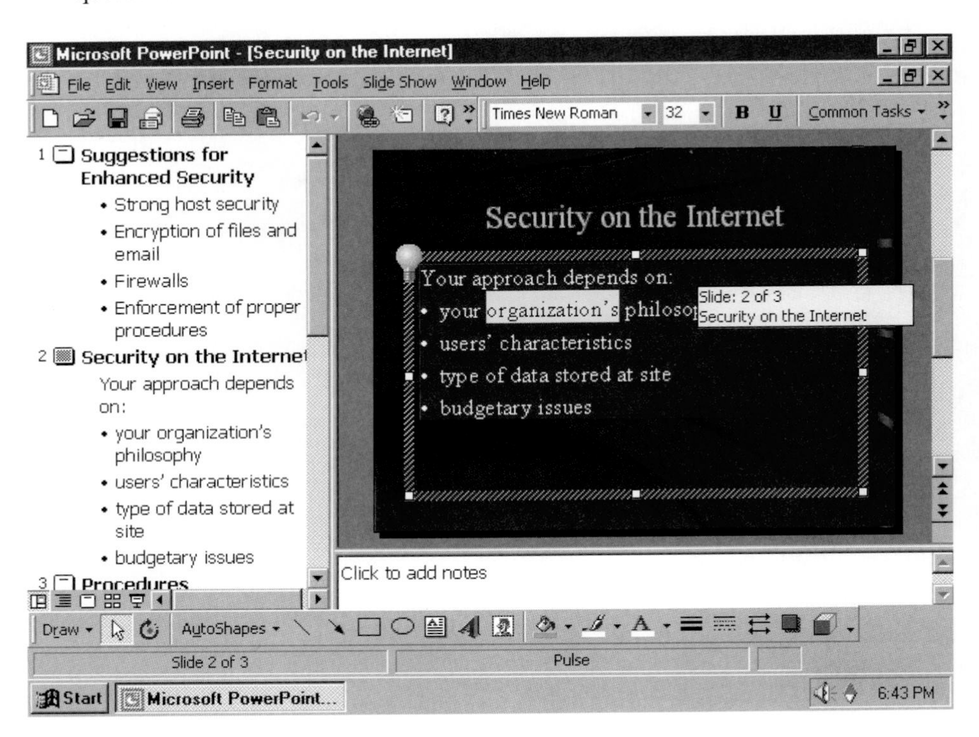

a. What is the name of the presentation?

b. What is the slide number? How many slides are in the presentation?

c. What action was taken to see the slide number and title at the right side of the screen?

d. The text *organization's* is highlighted. If you begin typing *site's,* what happens to the highlighted text?

e. Which box is the text area or placeholder?

f. Which box is the title area or placeholder?

g. How do you move to the next slide?

h. Which button do you click to begin the show?

i. What view is showing?

2. Answer the following questions concerning a PowerPoint slide show:

a. What key do you press to move to the next screen in a show?

b. What key do you press to move back a screen?

c. What part of the screen do you select to view the pop-up menu that controls navigation in a show?

d. How can you exit a show and return to Normal View?

3. Suppose you are asked to edit an existing presentation. Start PowerPoint and make the following changes:

   a. Use the Office Assistant to get help on the topic: open an existing presentation.

   b. Open the presentation **Chap1-1**.

   c. Save under a new name, *Presenting a Show*, so that the original file remains unchanged.

   d. Edit slide 1 to replace the author's name with your own.

   e. Insert a new slide after the slide *Before an Audience*.

   f. Select the title placeholder and type *Over the Internet* as the slide title.

   g. Select the text placeholder and type *Presentation Conference Wizard* as the bulleted item.

   h. Move the last slide titled *On the Road* before *Over the Internet*. (Remember, you will need to change views.)

   i. Save your work.

   j. Run the show.

4. PowerPoint has many views.

   a. Open the presentation **Chap1-2** located on your student disk. Rename the file *Chat Rooms* to save the presentation under a new name. Create a new folder called *Internet Lecture*. Save the file *Chat Rooms* in the new folder.

   b. Select Microsoft Word Help in the Menu. Type PowerPoint views to explore topics related to these views. Select View PowerPoint Introduction, the online tutorial.

   c. Click the Show button in the Microsoft Help window. In the Index section, type *outline* to learn about importing an outline created in another program, such as Word.

   d. Close the Help window to return to the presentation. Click through the four slides. At Slide 2, click the lightbulb appearing on the slide to get hints or tips about PowerPoint.

5. Open the file **Chap1-3** on your student disk and save it as *New Features*. Edit the presentation as directed below.

   a. In slide 1, click on the title and edit so that it reads: *What's New In PowerPoint?* Click on the subtitle placeholder and enter your name.

   b. In slide 2, edit the second bulleted item to read: *PowerPoint Tutorial*. Change the bulleted item Options to read: *Handout Options*.

   c. Go to the last slide (should be slide 3) and add a new slide. Decide which auto layout should be selected. Enter as title, *New Features*. In the bulleted area, type: *New normal view—shows slides, outline and notes views in their own panes*.

   d. Add a fifth slide with the title: *All About Bullets*. In the bulleted area, type: *Use new styles and add your own customized bullets*.

   e. Go to Slide Sorter View and move slide 5, titled *All About Bullets*, so that it becomes slide 3 in your presentation.

   f. Save your work and run your show.

SUMMARY OF FUNCTIONS

Task	Mouse/Button	Menu	Keyboard
Beginning a slide show	Click the Slide Show View button	Slide Show, View or View, Slide Show	F5
Closing a presentation	Click the Close button	File, Close	[Alt] F
Ending a slide show	Click the triangle button and End Show		Esc
Go to [slide]	Click and drag the vertical scroll button		[number] + Enter
Inserting a new slide		Insert, New Slide	[Ctrl] M
Next slide in slide show	Click the triangle button and Next	Enter or PgDn	
Opening an existing presentation	Click the Open button	File, Open	[Ctrl] O
Previous slide in slide show	Click the triangle button and previous	PgUp	
Saving an existing presentation:			
Under current name	Click the Save button	File, Save	[Ctrl] S
Under new name		File, Save As	
Select views	Click a View button	View, Slide, Outline, Slide Sorter, or Notes Page	Alt +V

SELF-TEST PROBLEMS

True/False

Circle T for statements that are true and F for statements that are false.

T **F** **1.** A ToolTip identifies the options in a menu choice.

T **F** **2.** PowerPoint is a word processing program that provides the tools to create slides.

T **F** **3.** PowerPoint may be started through a shortcut icon or the Start button in the Windows taskbar.

T **F** **4.** A slide can be edited only in Slide view.

T F 5. The Office Assistant is an example of a floating toolbar.

T F 6. A file name is limited to eight characters or fewer and no spaces.

T F 7. When a slide is inserted in a presentation, it appears before the current slide.

T F 8. Objects on a slide can be text, pictures, or charts.

T F 9. When a slide is inserted, it must have the same layout as the preceding slide.

T F 10. Select Window, Slide Show to begin a presentation.

Multiple Choice

Select the best answer for each question and write the corresponding letter in the blank.

_______ **1.** Which PowerPoint view displays a single slide at a time for editing?
- **a.** Slide Sorter
- **b.** Slide
- **c.** Outline
- **d.** Slide Show

_______ **2.** Which is the first step in editing text in Slide view?
- **a.** Type in new text
- **b.** Press the Del key
- **c.** Click to select the text placeholder
- **d.** None of the above

_______ **3.** Which of the following commands are used to open an existing presentation?
- **a.** File, New
- **b.** File, Open
- **c.** File, Close
- **d.** File, Save

_______ **4.** Which of the following can be changed after inserting a slide?
- **a.** Its location in the presentation
- **b.** Its layout
- **c.** Neither of the above
- **d.** Both of the above

_______ **5.** What feature in PowerPoint gives another view of the slide you're working on?
- **a.** Office Assistant
- **b.** Common Tasks
- **c.** Slide Miniature
- **d.** None of the above

_______ **6.** In which view does the pop-up menu appear to offer navigational controls?
- **a.** Outline
- **b.** Slide Sorter
- **c.** Slide Show
- **d.** Slide

_______ **7.** Which feature is used to determine the slide number in Normal view?
- **a.** Status bar
- **b.** Formatting toolbar
- **c.** View buttons

d. View, Slide in the menu

_______ **8.** Which of the following commands is used to start a slide show?
a. Select File, Open
b. Select Window, New Show
c. Select Insert, Show
d. Select Slide Show, View Show

_______ **9.** Which view displays multiple slides and allows you to easily edit the slides?
a. Slide
b. Normal
c. Slide sorter
d. None of the above

_______ **10.** How do you move back a slide during a slide show?
a. Press PgUp
b. Press Enter
c. Mouse click
d. None of the above

Matching

Match each of the elements to the PowerPoint screen shown below with its resulting action.

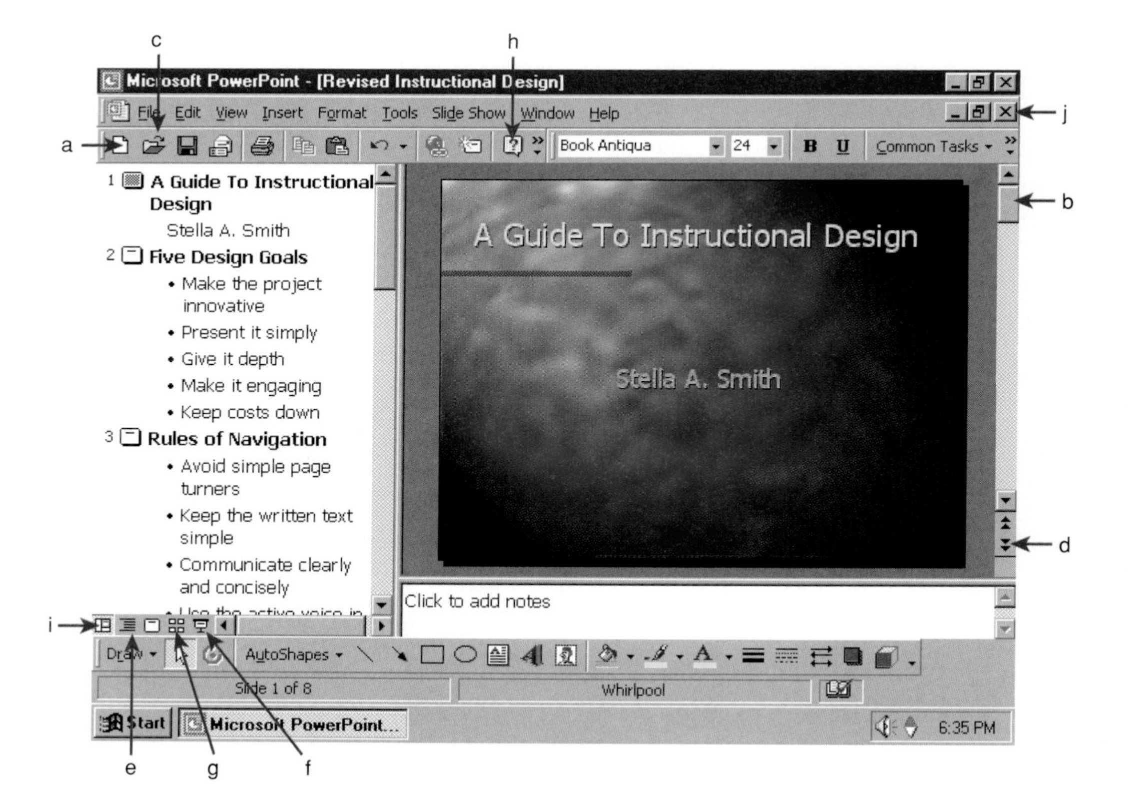

Click on	Action
_______	**1.** Opens an existing presentation
_______	**2.** Selects the Slide Sorter view
_______	**3.** Selects the Outline view
_______	**4.** Adds a new slide
_______	**5.** Selects Normal view
_______	**6.** Activates online help
_______	**7.** Moves to next slide
_______	**8.** Closes the presentation window
_______	**9.** Begins the slide show
_______	**10.** Slides up and down the presentation

Fill in the Blank

Fill in the blank with the missing word or phrase.

1. The _______ view shows the overall organization of a presentation.
2. The _______ in Help allows you to look up help topics by entering a selected topic.
3. The _______ _______ view provides the easiest way to rearrange slides.
4. The _______ button can be used to open an existing presentation or the _______ _______ menu selections can be used to open a presentation.
5. To begin a show, click the _______ _______ button in the bottom left side of the window.
6. Besides a computer slide show, PowerPoint can be used to create _______ or _______.
7. When a toolbar appears someplace other than at the top or around the edges of a window, it is called a _______.
8. Click the _______ _______ button in the vertical scroll bar to move from one slide to another in Slide view.
9. The _______ toolbar contains buttons that change text appearance.
10. In the Slide Show view, press _______ or _______ to go to the next slide.

ANSWERS

True/False: 1. F 2. F 3. T 4. F 5. T 6. F 7. F 8. T 9. F 10. F

Multiple Choice: 1. b 2. c 3. b 4. d 5. c 6. c 7. a 8. d 9. d 10. a

Matching: 1. c 2. g 3. e 4. a 5. i 6. h 7. d 8. j 9. f 10. b

Fill in the Blank: 1. Outline 2. Index 3. Slide Sorter 4. Open; File, Open 5. Slide Show 6. slides, overheads 7. floater 8. Next slide 9. Formatting 10. PgDn, Enter

Creating a Presentation

OUTLINE

Using a Template to Create a Presentation
Entering Text in Outline View
Reorganizing the Outline
Self-Correcting Features
Editing Text
Moving Text and Slides
Changing Text Appearance
Changing Fonts and Font Sizes
Modifying Bullets
Printing a Presentation
Strengthening Your Skills
Summary of Functions
Self-Test Problems and Answers

LEARNING OBJECTIVES

After completing this chapter, you will be able to

- Use a template to create a presentation
- Enter text in Outline view
- Rearrange slides in Outline view
- Use spelling checker, AutoCorrect, and Style Checker
- Format text
- Edit an existing slide
- Format a bulleted list
- Print a presentation

Using a Template to Create a Presentation

To create a presentation, PowerPoint provides three approaches: the **AutoContent Wizard**, the **Design Template**, and the **blank presentation**. The design template lies between the AutoContent Wizard (maximum help) and the Blank Presentation (no help).

PowerPoint gives you the option of two different templates: **Presentation Templates** (color scheme and outline text, which you edit) and **Design Templates** (color scheme, no outline text). You will use a **Design Template** to provide a color scheme and a "look" for your slides while you type in text as directed in this lesson.

1. Select **File, New** in the menu. The PowerPoint dialog box appears (Figure 2.1).
2. Click **Design Templates, OK**.
3. Click the **Design Templates tab** in the New Presentation dialog box and click **Ribbons**. Notice in Figure 2.2 the preview of that template appears on the screen also. Click **OK** to select this template.
4. Leave the default setting of Title Slide and click **OK**.

(continued on page 46)

FIGURE 2.1
The PowerPoint Dialog Box

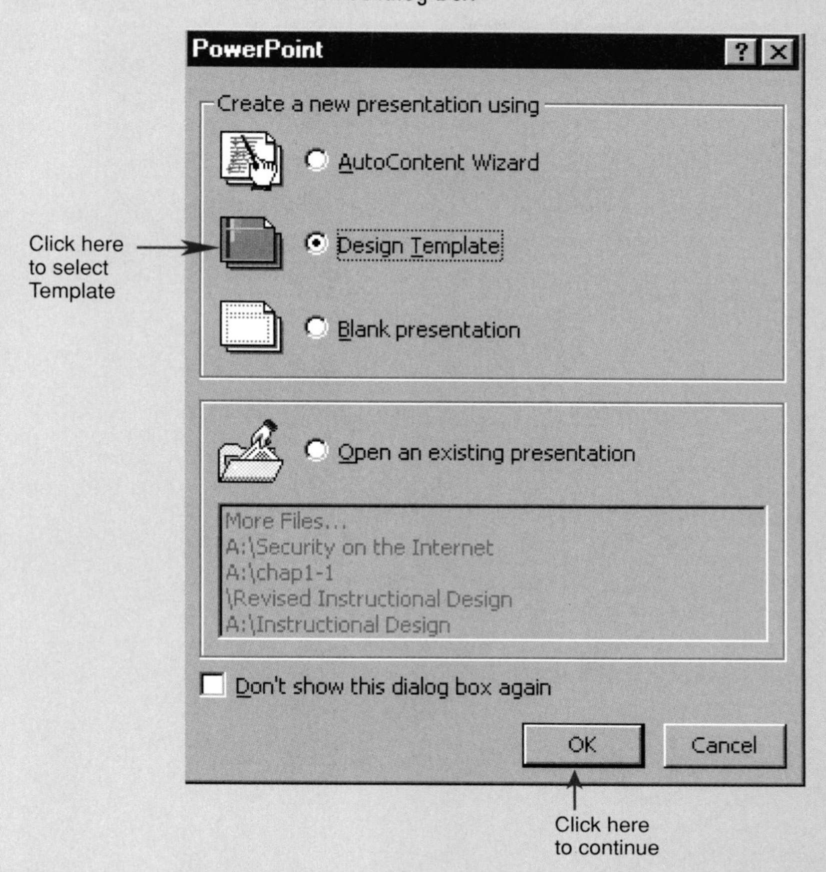

FIGURE 2.2
Presentation Templates

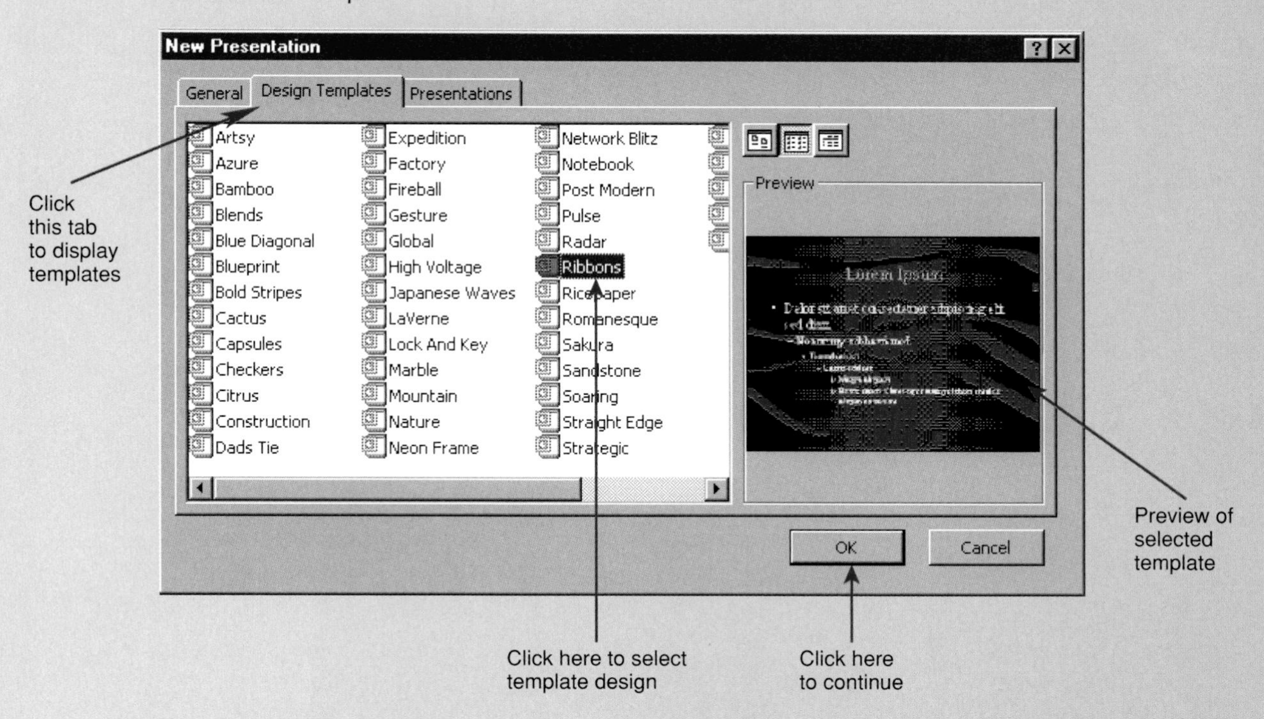

Using a Template to Create a Presentation (continued)

5. Click in the **Title placeholder** and type **Designing for the Screen**. Refer to Figure 2.3.
6. Click in the **Subtitle placeholder** and type **Karen Brown**.
7. Press **Enter** to go to the next line and type **Instructional Designer**.
8. **Save your file** to wherever your student files are stored. Name your file **Designing for the Screen**.

FYI **PowerPoint Dialog Box**

The dialog box is available only when you *first* start PowerPoint. Once you close this window, you will not see it again until the next time you start PowerPoint.

FIGURE 2.3
Title Slide

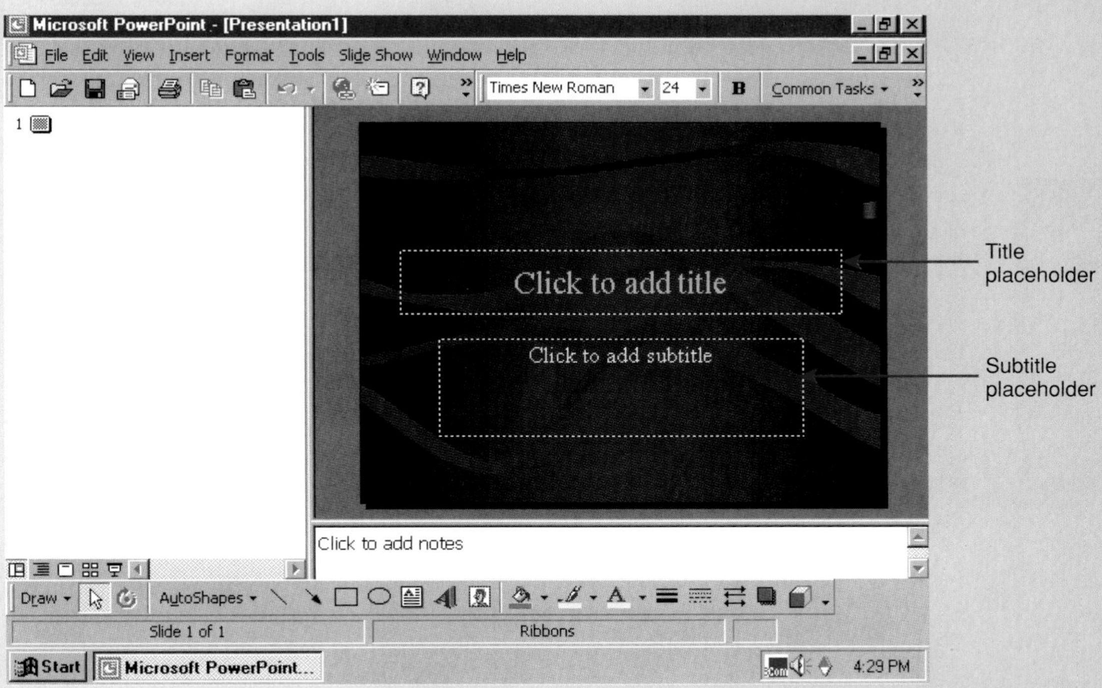

Title placeholder

Subtitle placeholder

Entering Text in Outline View

If you are not in the file Designing for the Screen that you began in the previous lesson, open the file. In this lesson, you will work in Normal view to continue creating slides for this new presentation.

1. Click **View, Toolbars** in the menu and select the **Outlining toolbar**. The toolbar will appear on the left side of your screen.
2. Click the **New Slide button** to add the next slide.
3. The New Slide dialog box appears. Notice the Bulleted List is set by default because this normally follows a title slide. Click **OK**.
4. Repeat steps 2 and 3. Type **The Function of Color**. Press Enter.
5. Type **Focus attention**.
6. Select the third slide by clicking the slide icon to the left of it, as shown in Figure 2.4.
7. Press the **Demote** button on the Outline toolbar. This line of text now becomes part of the previous slide. It is a bulleted item because this layout has a bulleted list for the second placeholder.
8. Click at the end of this first bulleted item and press Enter to continue the bulleted list. Refer to Figure 2.5 for the remaining items.

(continued on page 50)

FIGURE 2.4
Demotion of a Slide

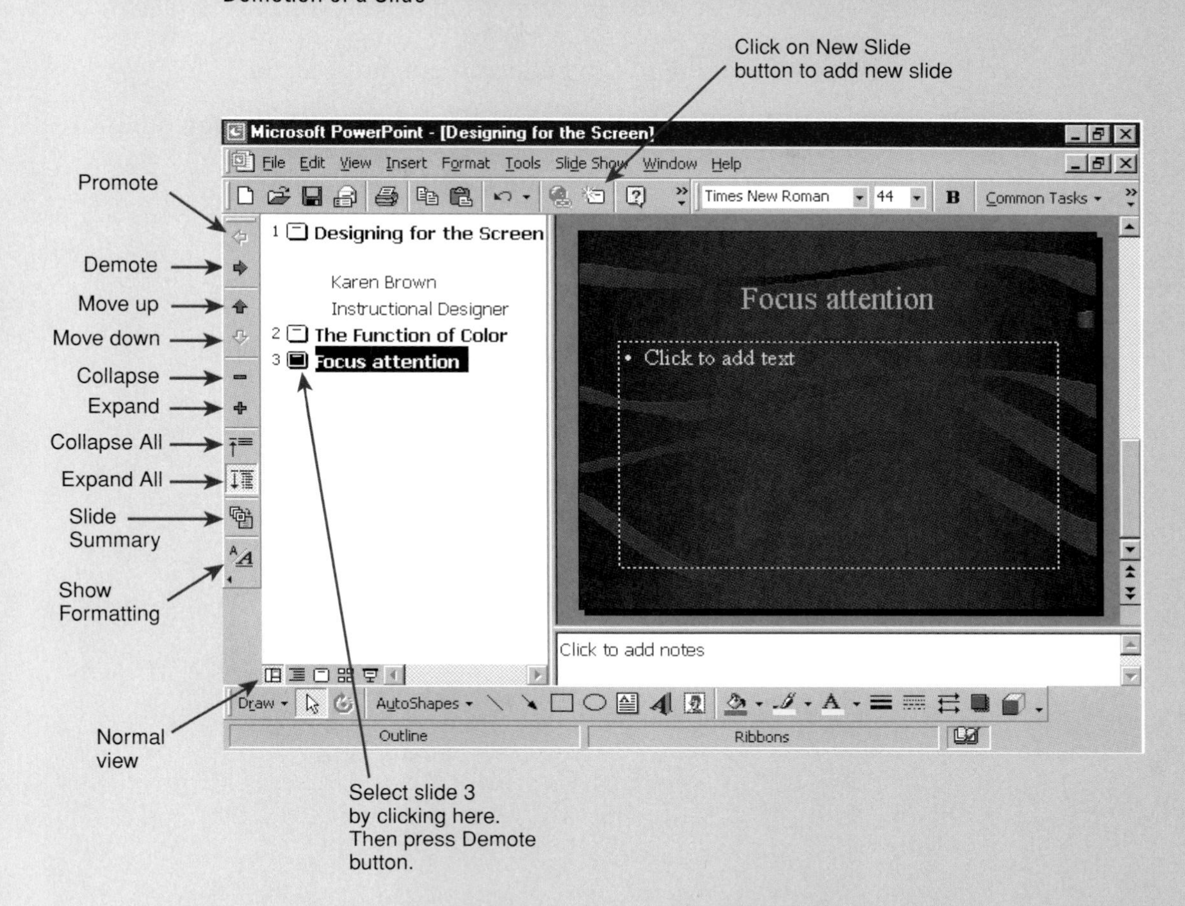

FIGURE 2.5
Additional Bulleted Items

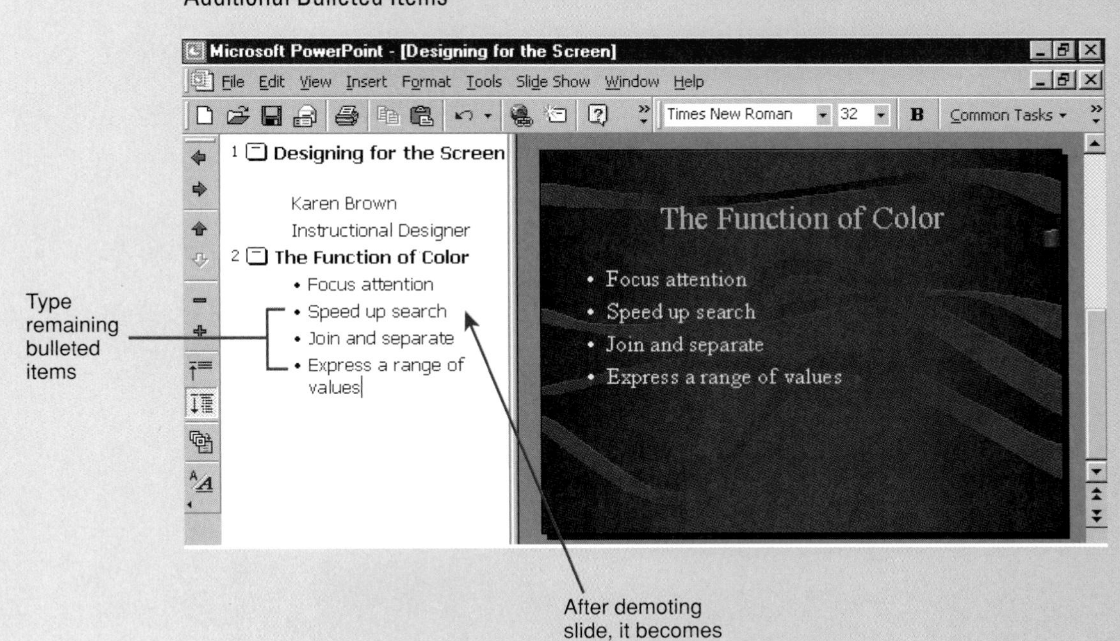

Entering Text in Outline View (continued)

9. At the end of the fourth bulleted item, press Enter.
10. Press **Tab**. This is another way to demote text. Type **Temperatures from blue to red**. Press Enter.
11. Click the **Promote button** on the Outline toolbar to move the next line of text up one level in the outline, as shown in Figure 2.6. Pressing the Shift + Tab keys also promotes text.
12. Type **Avoid unnecessary color**. Save your work.

FIGURE 2.6

Promotion of a Slide

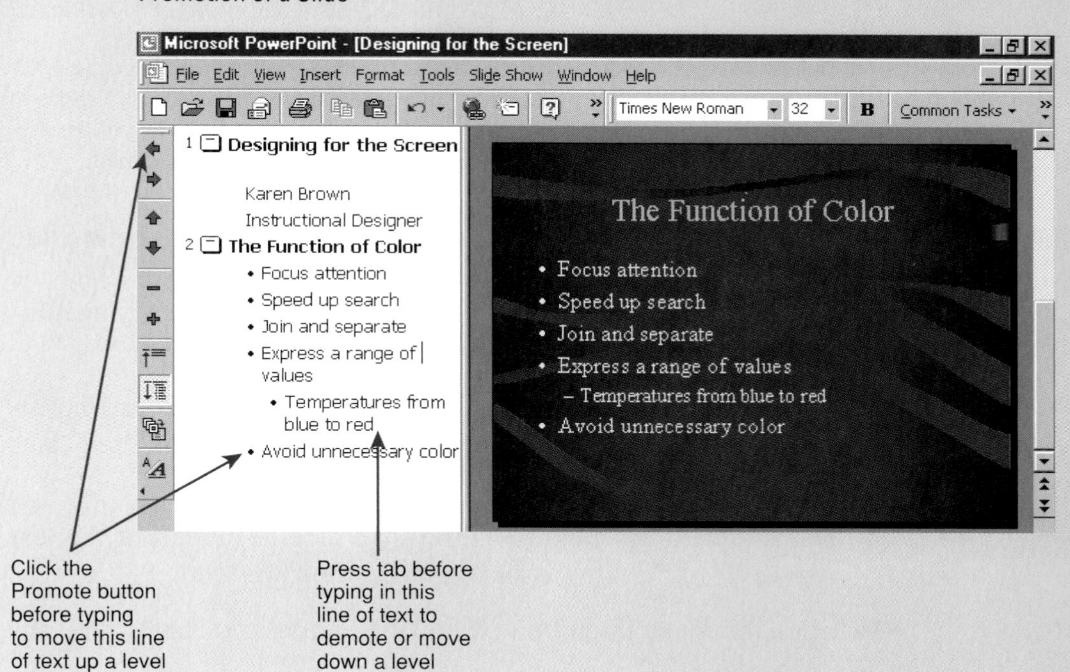

NOTES

Importing Text from Other Documents

You can use existing text from another document although it must be set up as an outline. For instance, a heading 1 becomes a slide title, a heading 2 becomes the first level of text, and so on. If there are no styles in the document, PowerPoint uses the paragraph indents to create an outline. An existing Word outline is especially simple to import. Open the document in Word, select File, Send To and then click Microsoft PowerPoint.

WARNING

Too Many Bullets?

Pressing Enter one time too many may result in an extra bullet. Just press the Backspace key to delete an unwanted bullet.

TIP

How Many Levels of Text?

Although PowerPoint allows you to create several levels of text on a slide, it is best to limit yourself to no more than three levels, using the third level sparingly. Keep the slide text simple and short.

Reorganizing the Outline

Once some text has been entered into your outline, you can rearrange the order and change the view of your outline. In this lesson you will add more slides to your presentation and learn how to edit the outline. You should be in the presentation Designing for the Screen in Normal View to begin this lesson.

1. Click on the **Outline View button**. Click the **New Slide button** to add another slide. Use the Bullet layout. Enter the content of slide 3 from Figure 2.7. Repeat for slide 4. (Type as indicated, even with spelling error.)
2. Click the **Collapse All button** on the Outline toolbar. The detail beneath the slides is hidden, but a wavy, gray line indicates there's something there.
3. Select slide 4 by clicking on the slide icon to the left of the text *The Value of Pictures* as shown in Figure 2.8.
4. Click the **Move Up button** on the Outline toolbar.
5. Slide 4 now becomes slide 3 in the presentation.

(continued on page 54)

FIGURE 2.7
Slides 3 and 4

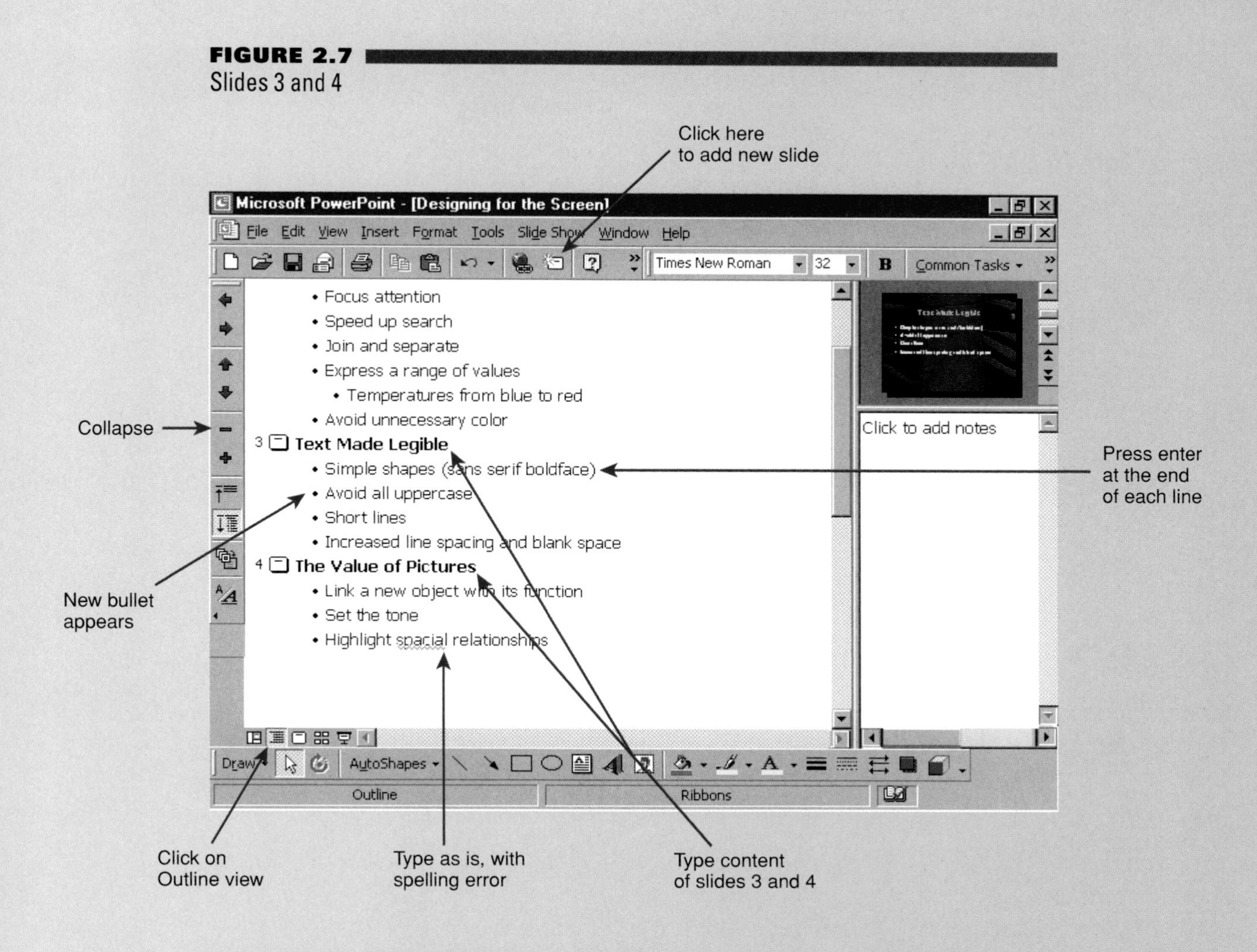

FIGURE 2.8
Slide Selected for Move

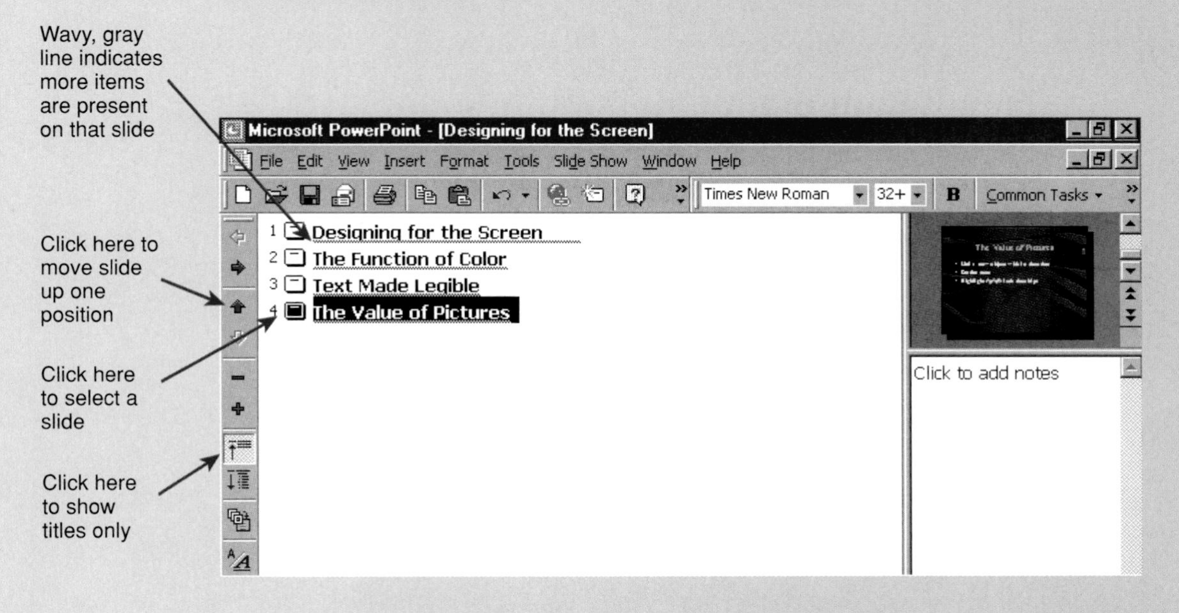

Reorganizing the Outline (continued)

6 Select slide 2. Click the **Expand button** in the Outline toolbar. As shown in Figure 2.9, only slide 2 expands to show its bulleted items.

7 Click the **Expand All button** in the Outline toolbar to view all the bulleted items.

8 Click **Slide view** to view slides one at a time.

9 Click **Outline view** to return to your presentation outline. **Save** your work.

FYI The value of collapsing or expanding an outline lies in the complexity of your presentation. Collapsing an outline allows you to look at slide titles only and thus gain an appreciation of how well the presentation flows. Expanding an outline gives you a complete look at the depth of your presentation.

FIGURE 2.9
Expanded Slide

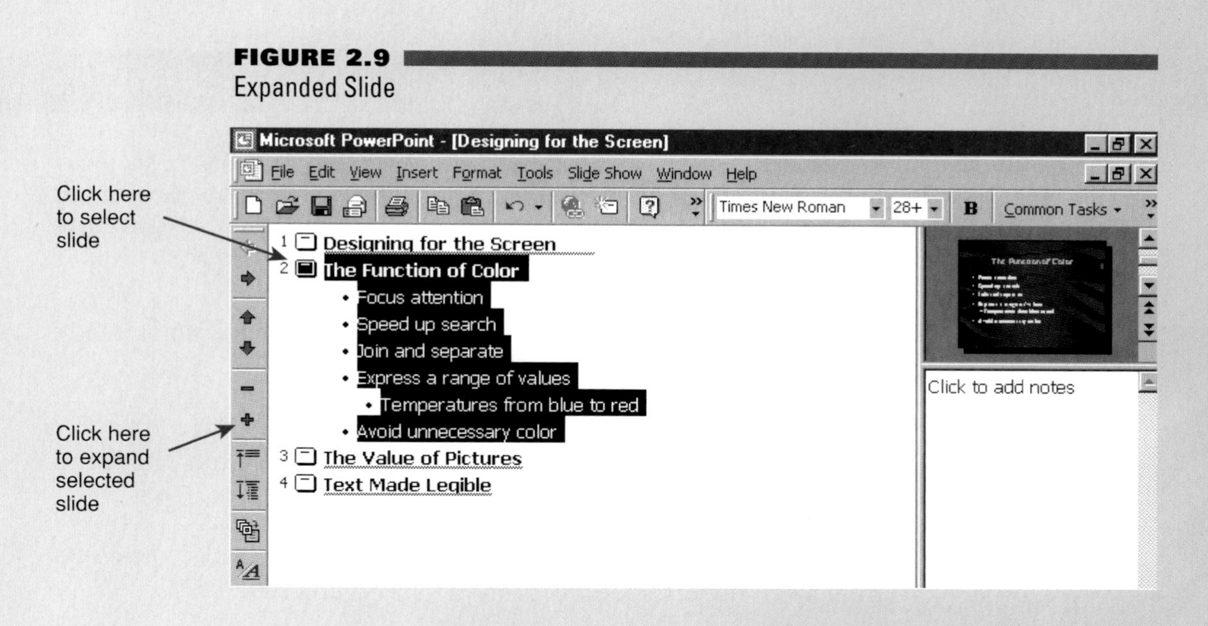

Self-Correcting Features

PowerPoint provides many of the same tools as can be found in the other **Office** applications to ensure error-free text. Tools such as AutoCorrect and Spelling/Style assist you in avoiding misspelled or mistyped words and grammatical errors. You will practice using these features in this lesson.

1. Open the file **Designing for the Screen** if you are not already there. Select **Outline view** .
2. When you typed in the final bulleted item in slide 3, you may have noticed a wavy red line appearing underneath the word *spacial.* PowerPoint alerts you to misspellings as you type.
3. Click your insertion point on the word *spacial* and right-click. Select the correct spelling as shown in Figure 2.10.
4. To check all the slides for spelling, click the **Spelling button** on the Standard toolbar. If the Spelling dialog box appears, click **ignore** if the word is spelled correctly.
5. If the word is spelled incorrectly, click on the correct spelling in the **Suggestions box** and click **Change**.
6. Click **OK** when a message appears telling you the spelling checker is complete.
7. Select **Tools, AutoCorrect** to view the AutoCorrect dialog box as shown in Figure 2.11. Click the scroll box to view the list of commonly mistyped words, which are automatically corrected by PowerPoint. Click the **Cancel button**.

(continued on page 58)

FIGURE 2.10
Check Spelling

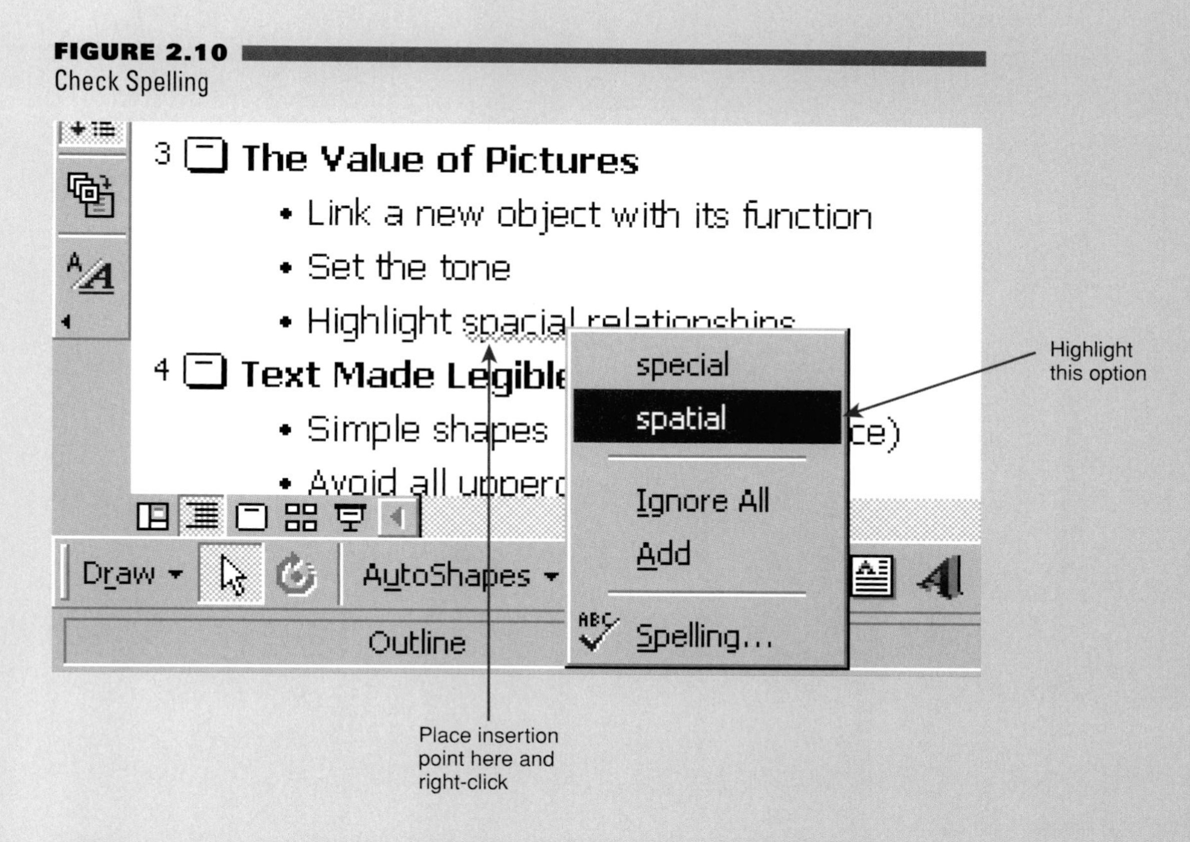

FIGURE 2.11
AutoCorrect Feature

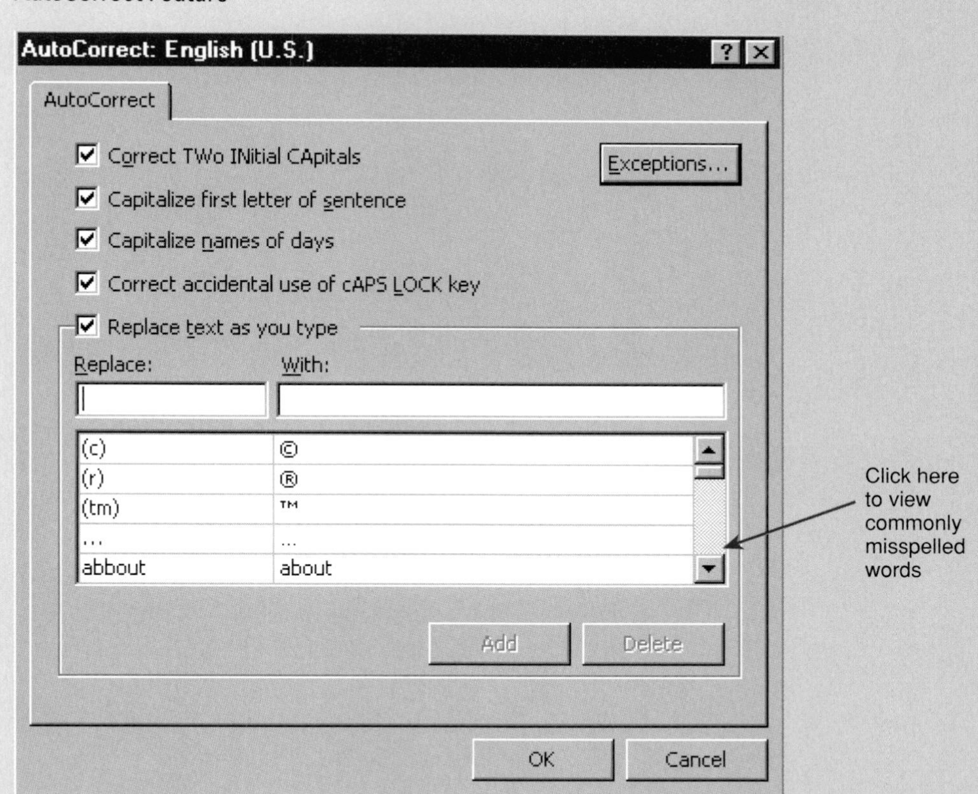

Self-Correcting Features (continued)

8. Select **Tools, Options, Spelling, and Style** to check the settings for a presentation's style.
9. Click the **Style Options button** to view settings. Click **Cancel** to return to your presentation. See Figure 2.12.
10. **Save** your work.

FIGURE 2.12
Style Checker

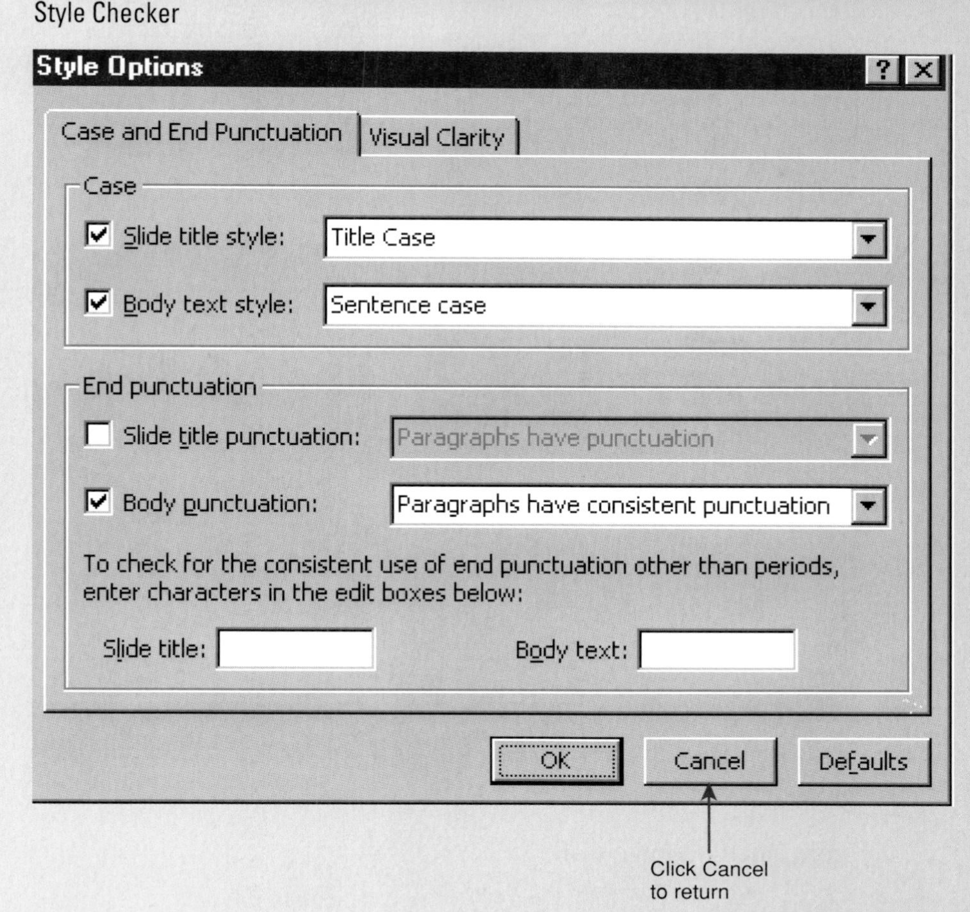

TIP

Customizing AutoCorrect

After perusing the list of typically mistyped words, you might want to include some of your own. Perhaps you often mistype a word. In the AutoCorrect dialog box, make sure the Replace text as you type check box is selected. In the Replace box, type mgiht to identify the word you typically mistype. In the With box, type the correct spelling—might. Then click Add and you've customized your list!

TIP

What Does the Lightbulb Do?

PowerPoint automatically checks your presentation for style. The lightbulb appears on your slide when a style or consistency issue arises. The lightbulb is not available if you turn off the Office Assistant. To turn on the Office Assistant, click Help in the menu and click Show Office Assistant.

Editing Text

Text editing in PowerPoint is similar to editing procedures in most word processing programs. You can delete characters by using the Backspace or Del keys. In this lesson, you will change text in Outline view, replace existing text with new text, and undo/redo your typing.

1. Place the flashing insertion point at the beginning of the line *Join and Separate.* Left-click and drag the insertion point across that bulleted item. You have selected this item for editing.
2. Type in **Differentiate and join**. This replaces the highlighted text.
3. Left-click and drag the flashing insertion point across the last bulleted item, **Avoid unnecessary color**, in slide 2. Press the **Del key** to remove this item and **Backspace** to remove the unwanted bullet.
4. Select **Edit** in the Menu toolbar. Click **Replace**. The Replace dialog box appears.
5. Type **boldface** in the **Find What** box.
6. Type **typeface** in the **Replace With** box. Refer to Figure 2.13 as a guide.

(continued on page 62)

FIGURE 2.13
Replace

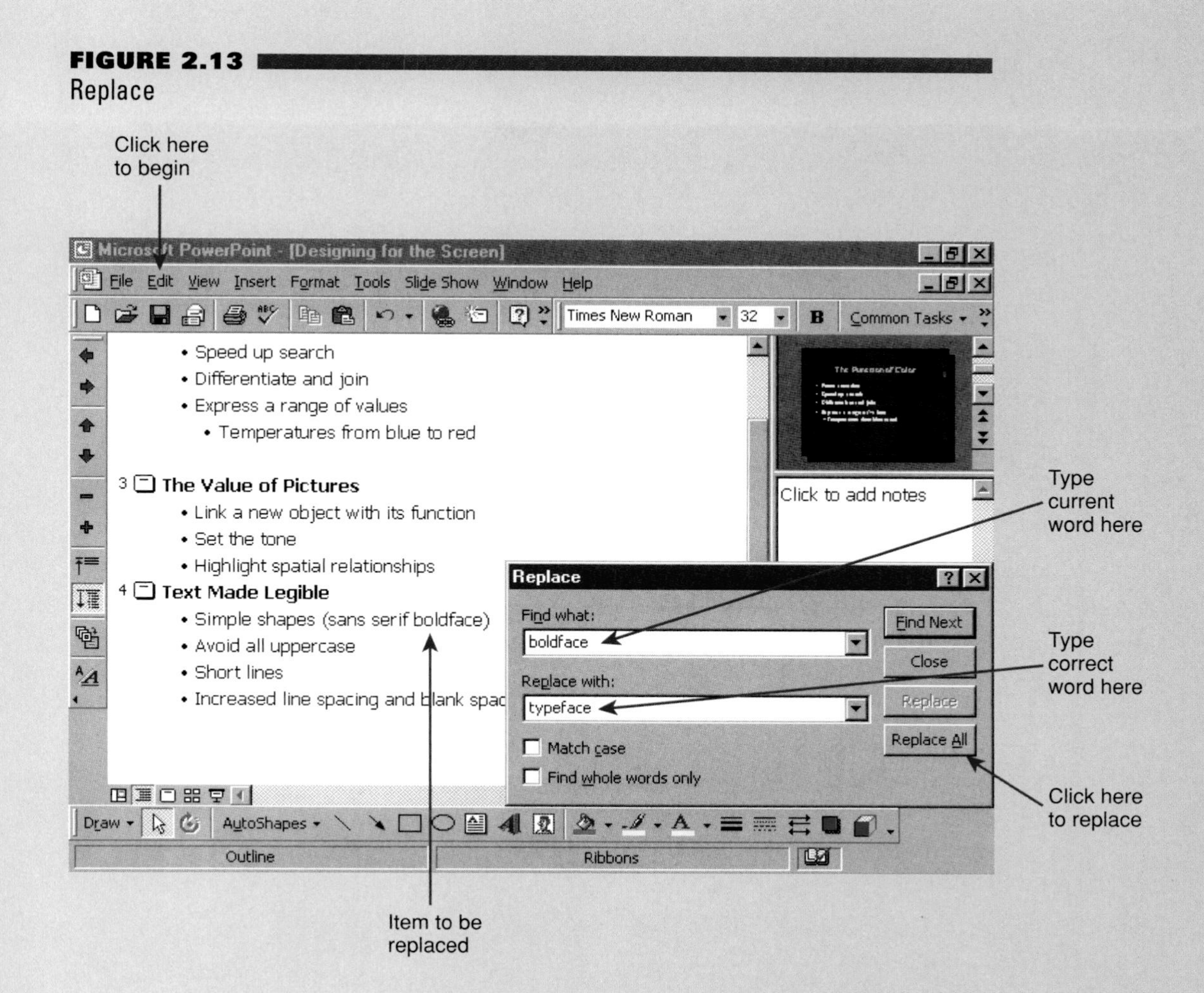

Editing Text (continued)

7 Click **Replace All**. A message will appear indicating the replacement has been made. Click **OK**. Click the **Close button** in the dialog box.

8 Click at the end of the line for the last bulleted item in **slide 4** and press **Enter** to add a bullet. Type in **Make an object recognizable** as shown in Figure 2.14.

9 Click the **Undo button** to remove your newest bulleted item.

10 Click **Redo** to bring back the bulleted item. You may need to click on More Buttons to view this button. **Save** your changes .

FIGURE 2.14
New Bulleted Item

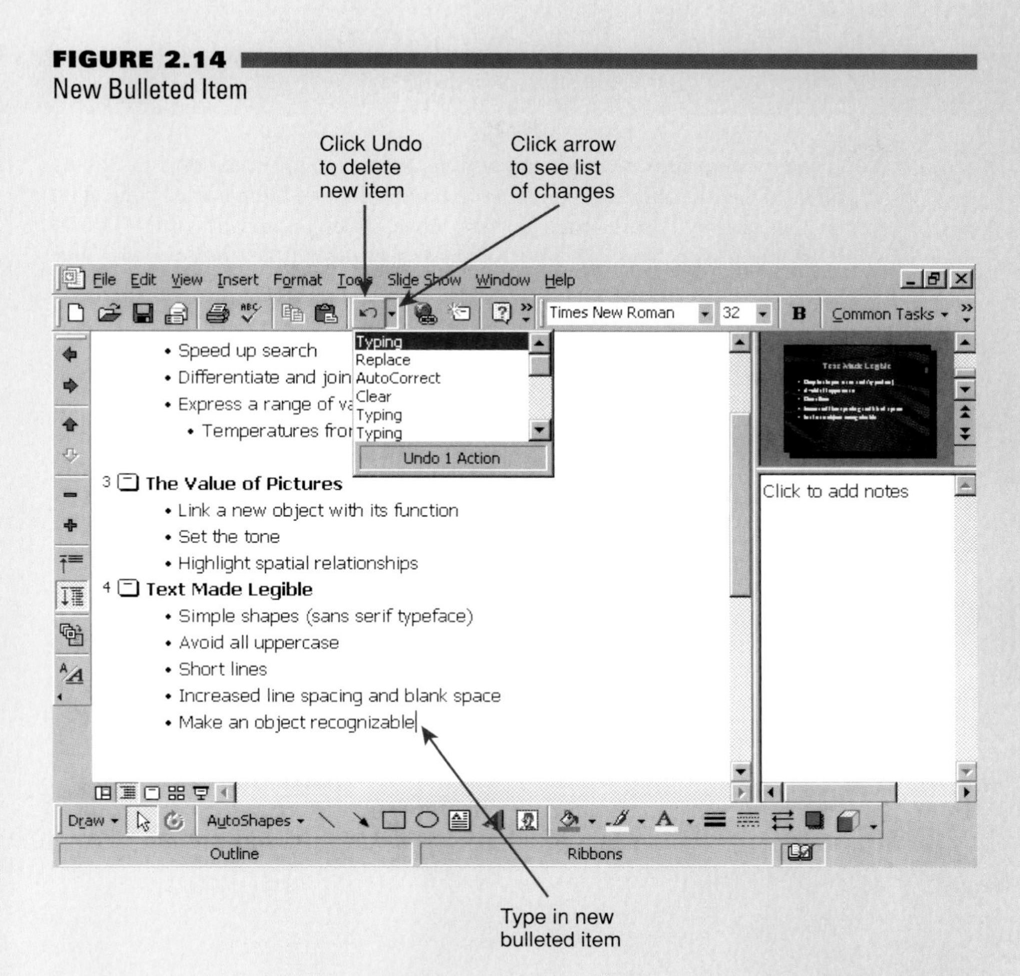

TIP

Using the Find Command

To find text, select Edit, Find in the Menu toolbar. Type whatever you want to find and click Find Next.

NOTES

Highlighting Text with the Keyboard

You can also highlight text using your keyboard. Place your insertion point to the left of the text you want to highlight. Press and hold the Shift key. To highlight one character, press the right arrow. To highlight one word at a time, press and hold Shift + Ctrl and then press the right arrow. To highlight one line, press and hold Shift + End or Shift + down arrow.

Moving Text and Slides

You have used various methods in previous lessons to move slides: in Chapter 1, you used the drag-and-drop method to move slides in Slide Sorter view; earlier in this chapter, you learned how to move slides up and down in Outline view. In this lesson, you will use the cut and paste buttons to move text and slides.

1. Open the file **Designing for the Screen** if you are not already there. Select **Slide view** and move to slide 4.
2. Click and drag your flashing insertion point across the final item in the bulleted list, as shown in Figure 2.15.
3. Click the **Cut button** on the Standard toolbar to delete this line of text from slide 4 and move it to the Clipboard.
4. Point to **slide 3** in your presentation. Click as shown in Figure 2.16 and press Enter to move to the next available line.

(continued on page 66)

FIGURE 2.15
Text Selected for Deletion

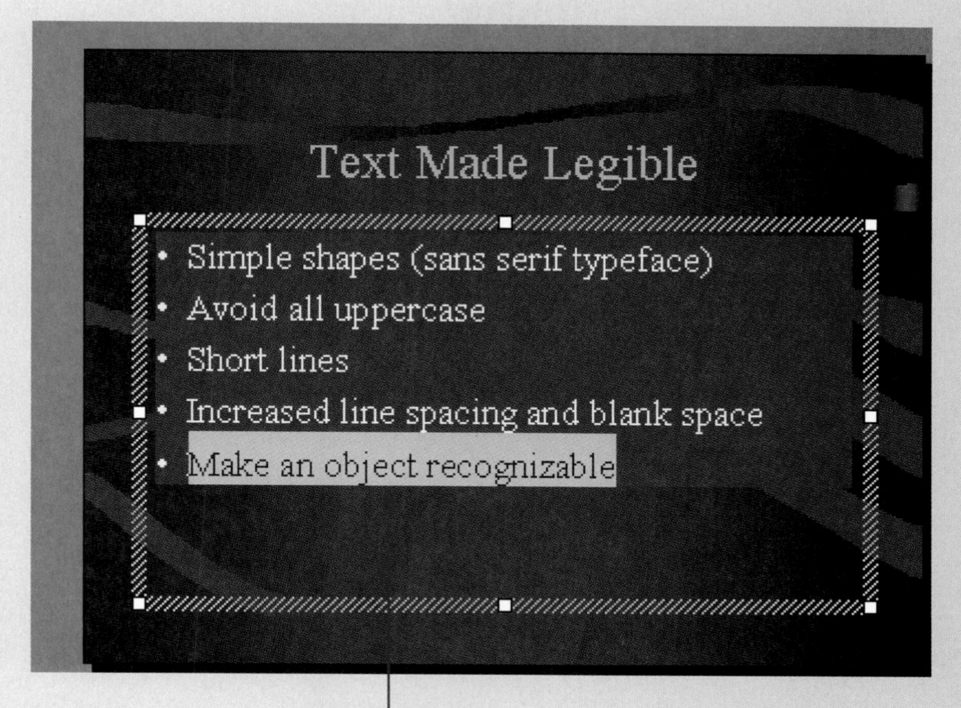

FIGURE 2.16
Bullet Added for New Text

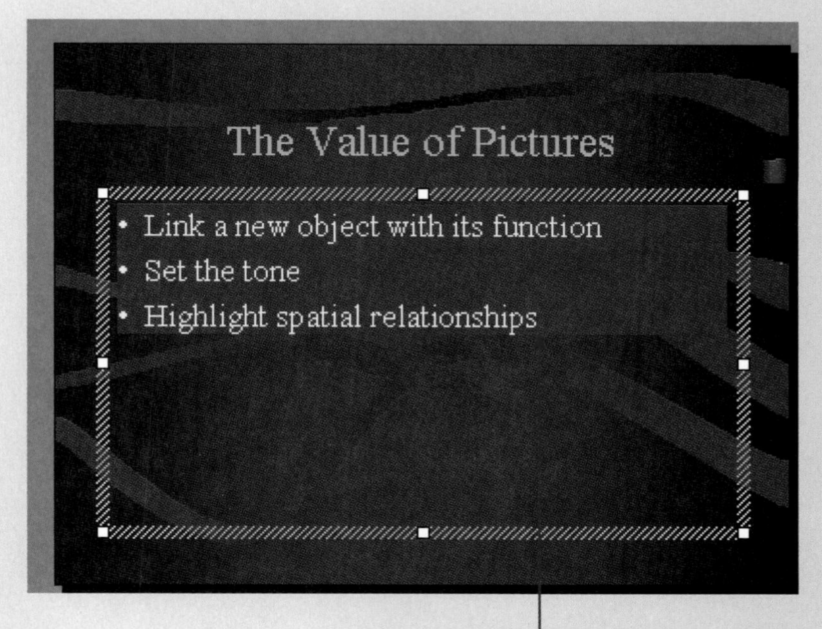

Moving Text and Slides (continued)

5. Click the **Paste button** on the Standard toolbar to display the bulleted item. Click outside the bulleted list placeholder to remove the editing box.
6. Select **Slide Sorter view** to easily move a slide from one position to another.
7. Click **slide 4** to select it. Notice the black border appears around the slide.
8. Click the **Cut button** to move it to the Clipboard. All that remains is a thin line as shown in Figure 2.17.
9. Select slide 1 and click the **Paste button** to move slide 4 into the new position of slide 2. Figure 2.18 shows the final slide sequence. **Save** your work.

FIGURE 2.17
Deleted Slide

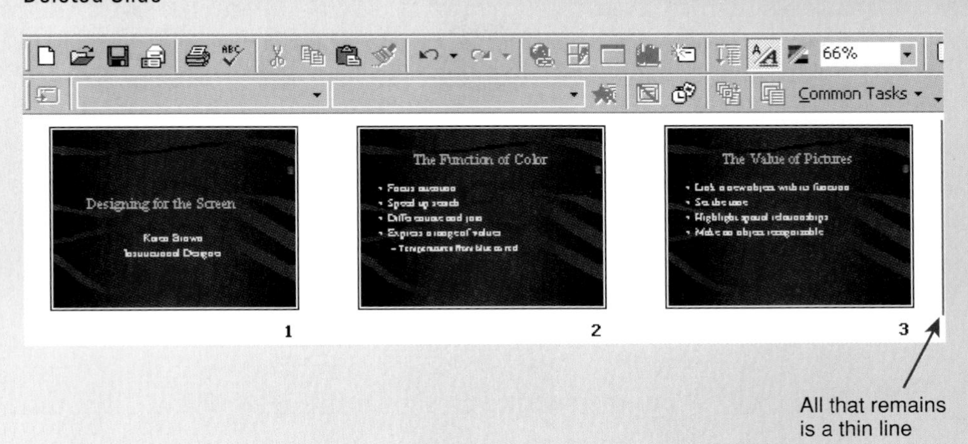

FIGURE 2.18
Pasted Slide

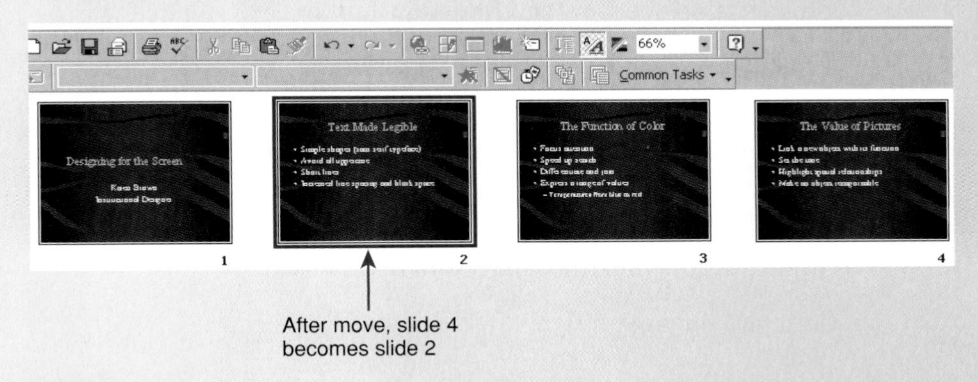

NOTES

The New Office Clipboard

The new Office Clipboard allows you to collect and paste up to 12 items from different programs with the Clipboard. After collecting items on the Clipboard, you can paste specific items or all the items. The Windows Clipboard you are working with on this page is separate from the Office Clipboard.

TIP

Keyboard Shortcuts for Cut and Paste

Select the text to be moved, and press Ctrl + C. Move the insertion point to where you want the text pasted, and press Ctrl + V.

Changing Text Appearance

After entering text, you may decide to highlight some of the words. You can highlight text by adding boldface, italic, underline, and shadow. You can add these features through the buttons available on the Formatting toolbar. You can change text color with the Font Color button on the Drawing toolbar. To line up text exactly the way you want it, you can use the Alignment buttons on the Formatting toolbar.

1. Open the file **Designing for the Screen** if you are not already there. Select **Slide view** .
2. At slide 1, select the subtitle as shown in Figure 2.19. Click the **Bold button** on the Formatting toolbar.
3. Make sure the subtitle is still selected. Look at the Formatting toolbar to find the **Center Alignment button** . Notice it is already selected. Do not change the setting.
4. Select the title of slide 1. Click the **Shadow button** . The text now has a small shadow, giving the title more depth.
5. Go to slide 2 and highlight the word **Avoid** to select it, as shown in Figure 2.20. Click the **Underline button** .

(continued on page 70)

FIGURE 2.19
Bold Text

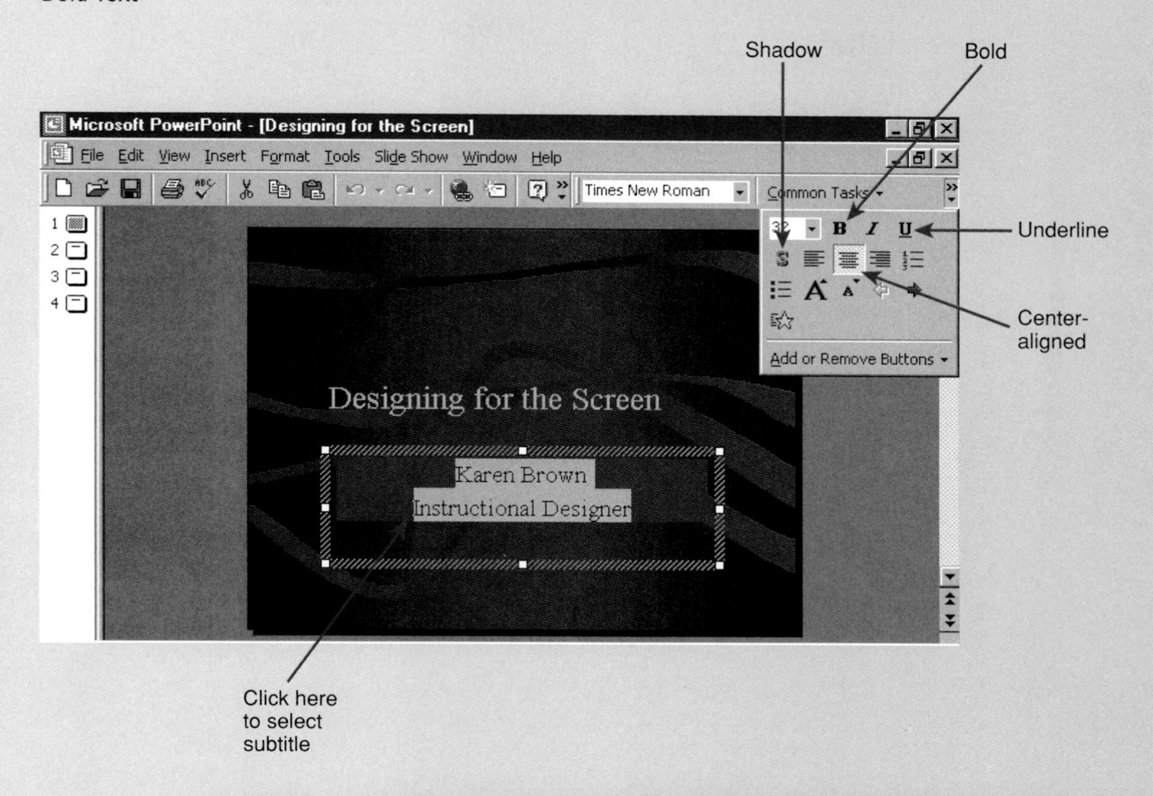

FIGURE 2.20
Underlined Text

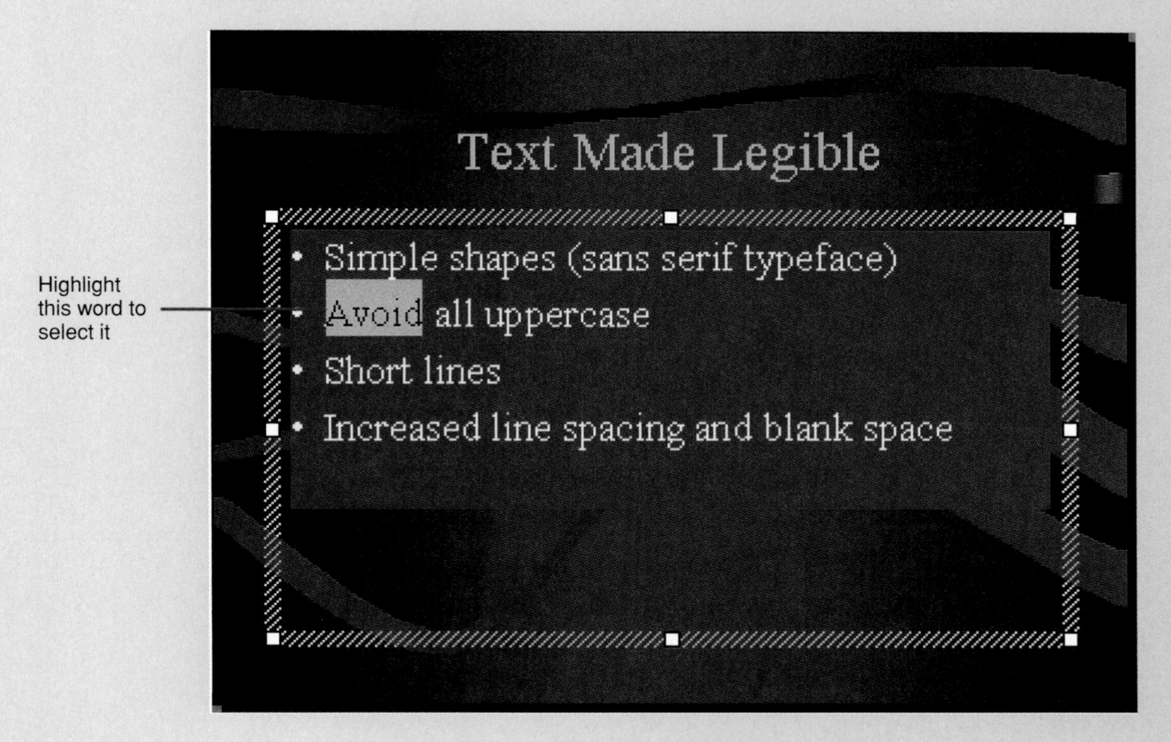

Changing Text Appearance (continued)

6. Go to **slide 3** and click the text as shown in Figure 2.21.
7. Click the **Font Color down arrow** on the Drawing toolbar.
8. Click **More Font Colors**. Click the designated color as shown in Figure 2.21. Click OK.
9. Click outside the editing box to view the colored text.
10. Save your work.

FYI When you use the **Alignment buttons**, text is aligned **inside its text block.** If you want to move the text block, you must first click it so that the hashed border appears. Make sure your pointer changes shape to a four-headed black arrow. Hold down the mouse button and drag the block to its new location.

FIGURE 2.21
Colored Text

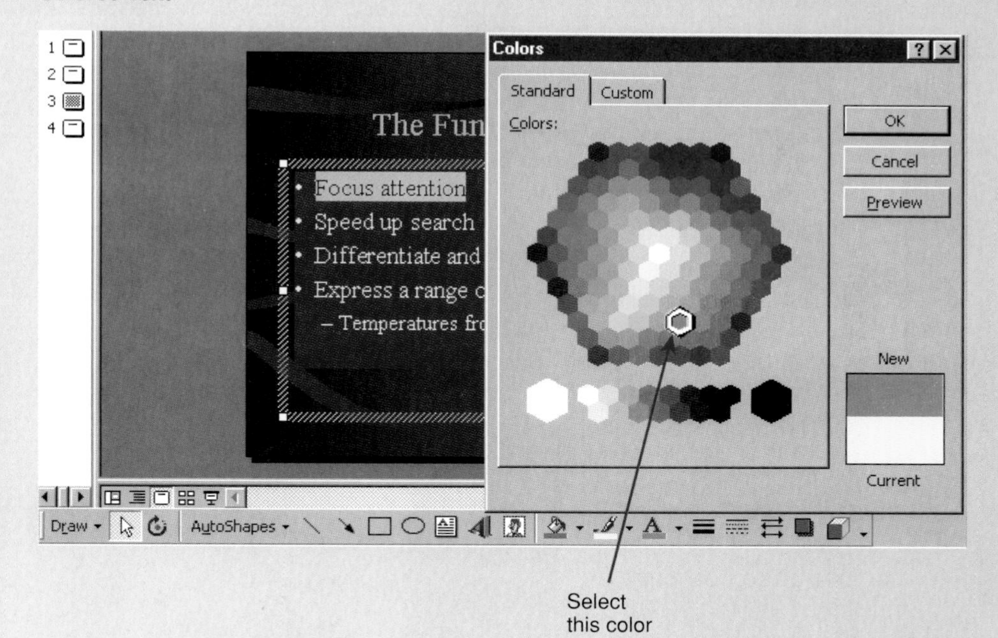

NOTES

The Format Painter

This tool found in PowerPoint allows you to copy a style (a style including formatting such as bold, underline, and text color) from selected text to other text. First, select the text that contains the style to be copied. Click the Format Painter button on the Standard toolbar and then drag it across the text where you want to apply the style.

TIP

Toggle Buttons

The attribute buttons like Bold, Italic, Underline, and Shadow are called toggles. You click a toggle to turn on a feature; click again to turn it off.

Changing Fonts and Font Sizes

Fonts are effective at conveying a certain tone to your document. A **font** is a group of characters that share a similar design or typeface. Some fonts are whimsical or light-hearted while others are more professional or conservative in appearance. The size of a font is referred to as its **point size**. The higher the point size, the bigger the character is. In this lesson, you will learn how easy it is to change fonts.

1. Open the file **Designing for the Screen** if you are not already there. You should be at the **Slide view**.
2. At slide 1, select the title and click the **Font drop-down arrow** and click the font as shown in Figure 2.22.
3. Change the font size by clicking on the **Font Size drop-down arrow** and click the font size as shown in Figure 2.23.

(continued on page 74)

FIGURE 2.22
Font

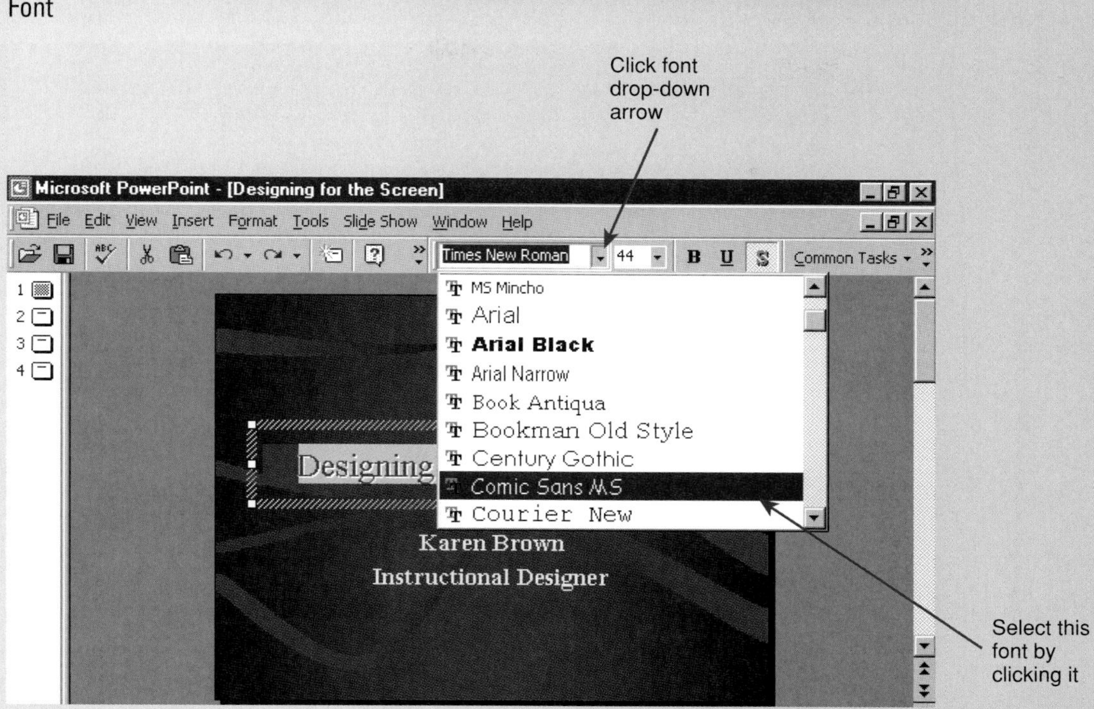

FIGURE 2.23
Font Size

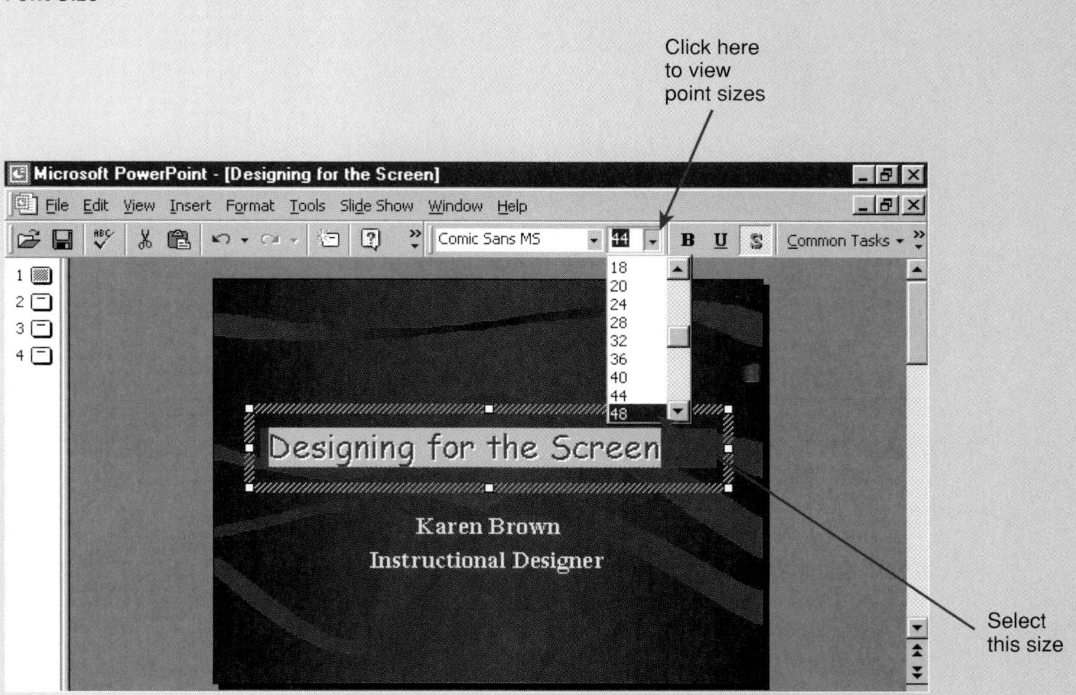

Changing Fonts and Font Sizes (continued)

4. Click the subtitle as shown in Figure 2.24 and select the same font.

5. Click the **Increase Font Size button** to increase the font size to 36 pt. The **Increase and Decrease Font Size buttons** allow you to see the impact of your choice immediately.

6. **Save** your changes.

FIGURE 2.24
Increase Font Size Button

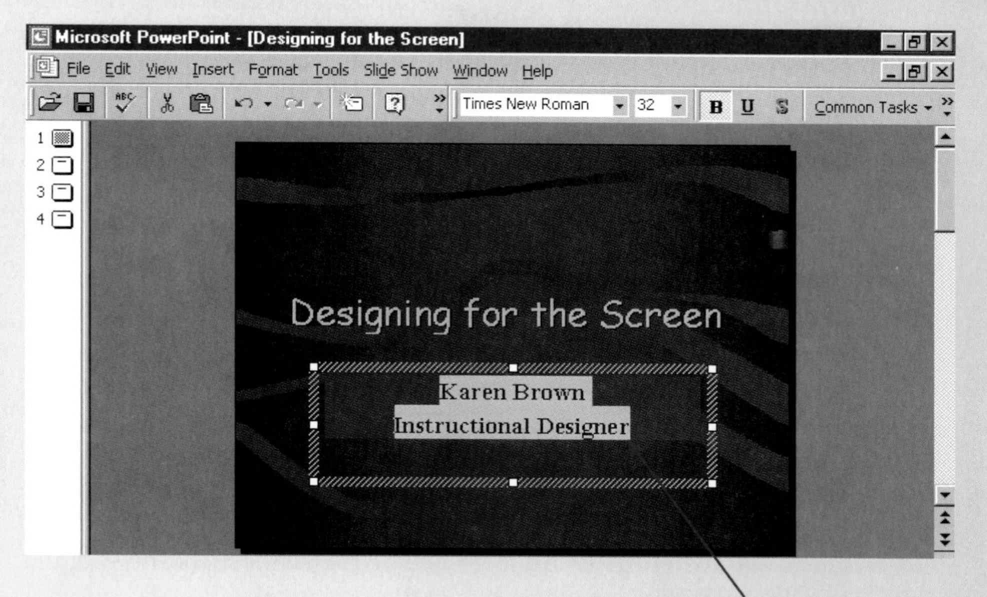

TIP

Font Talkin'

Font sizes may appear different although they are identical in point size. For instance, a 12-point Times New Roman appears smaller than the 12-point Bookman Old Style font. This is because some typefaces spread out more than others.

WARNING

Impact of Font Changes

If you change a font on a slide, this change will not affect other slides in the presentation. To change a font for all the slides, the font must be changed on the Slide Master. To change the Slide Master, select View, Master, Slide Master. Make the desired changes to a selected text area; these changes will impact the text on all slides.

Modifying Bullets

When you select a design template, the bullet style is selected for you. You may decide, however, to change the bullet symbol to draw attention to your message or fit in with the theme or tone of your presentation. You can also adjust the distance between the bullet and its accompanying text. To change all the bullets simultaneously, you will edit from the Master Slide.

1. Open the file **Designing for the Screen** if you are not already there. You should be at **Slide view.**
2. Click **View, Master, Slide Master**. Your Slide Master appears as shown in Figure 2.25. Click the first line in the **Object Area**.
3. Select **Format, Bullets** and **Numbering** in the menu.
4. Click the **check mark** symbol as shown in Figure 2.26.
5. Click **OK** to return to Slide Master. You can see the new bullet style, which impacts all bullets at the first level.
6. Click the **Close button** to exit the Slide Master. Click the **Next Slide button** to see the impact of the new bullet style.

(continued on page 78)

FIGURE 2.25
Master Slide

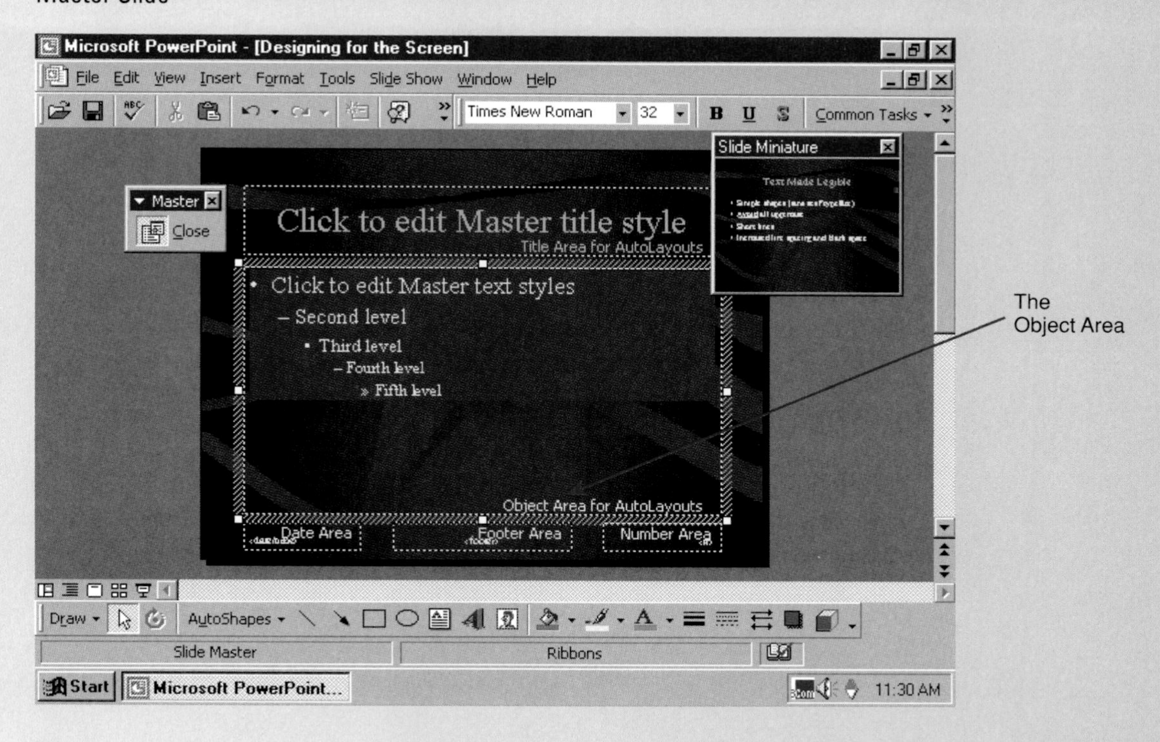

FIGURE 2.26
Select Bullet Shape

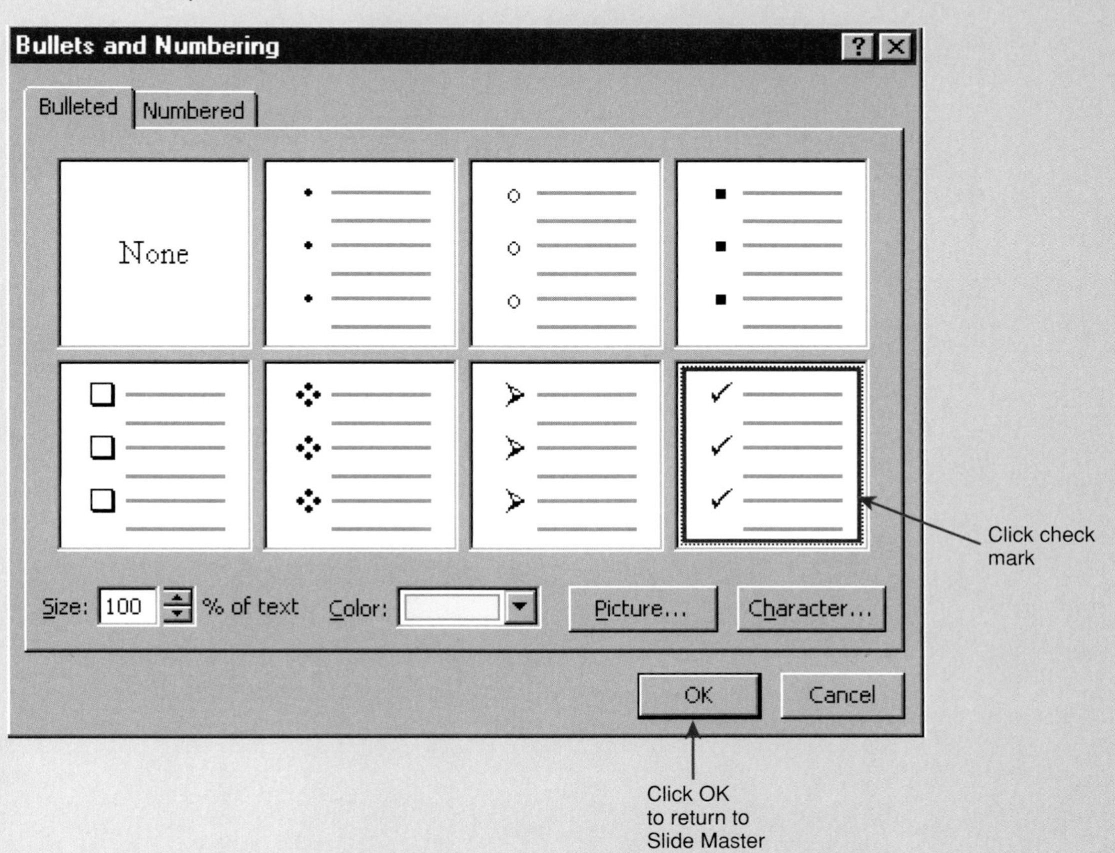

Modifying Bullets (continued)

7 The bullets and text are quite close together. To change the distance between bullets and text, click **View, Master, Slide Master** to change the indents. Make sure the ruler appears by selecting **View, Ruler** in the menu.

8 Click inside the Object Area before the word **Click**.

9 Drag the **indent markers** on the ruler to the position as shown in Figure 2.27.

10 Click the **Close button** to return to the slides. Select **View** and click **Ruler** so that the ruler no longer appears on the screen. Review your slides to see the impact of your latest change. **Save** your work.

FIGURE 2.27
Modified Indent for Bullets

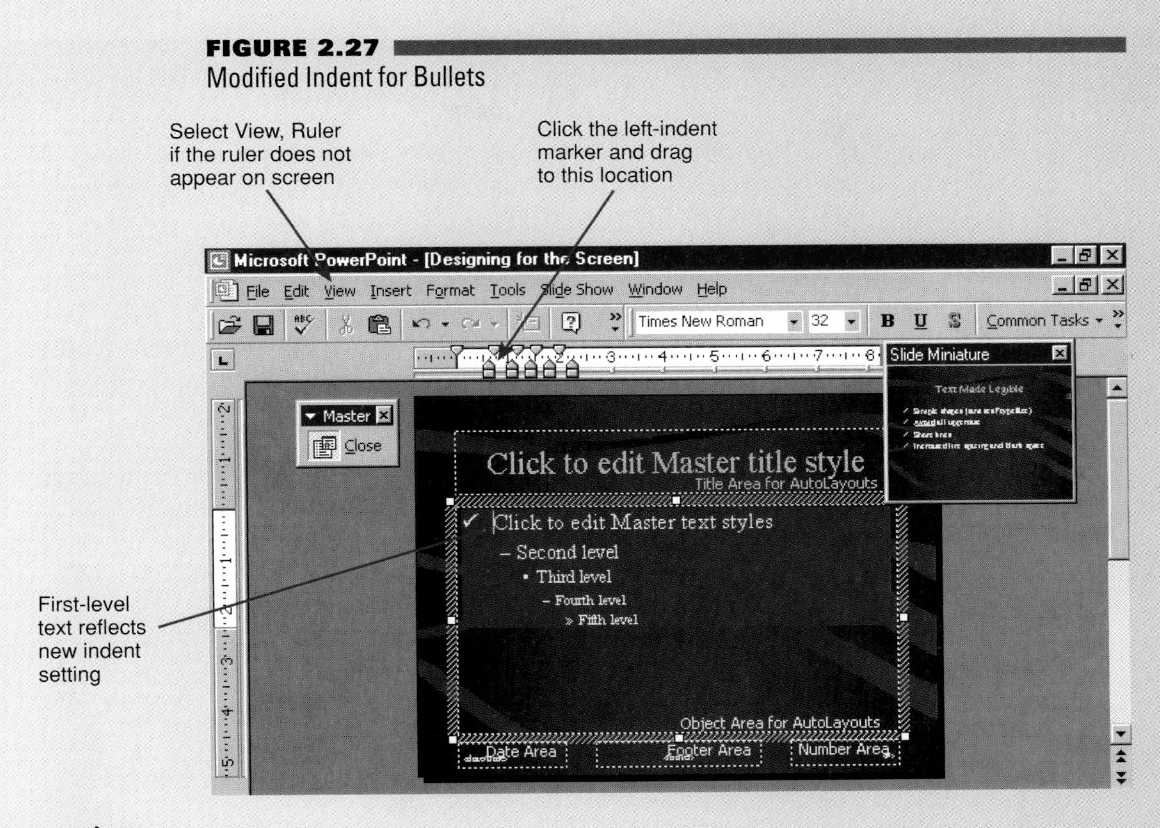

NOTES

More about the Slide Master

The Slide Master can be viewed as being like any slide. You can add pictures, styles, text, and borders, thus affecting every slide in your presentation, or simply add these features to slides individually. The most important elements in the Slide Master are the Title Area and the Object Area. The Title Area contains the formatting guide for each slide's title. The Object Area establishes the look of bulleted lists, including the bullet itself, as well as the styles, sizes, and indents for each item in the list.

TIP

Bullets Made Easy

Buttons on the Formatting toolbar can assist you with some of the modifications you might make on bullets. Clicking the Bullets button when you have clicked on a bulleted item will delete the bullet. Similarly, clicking on an item and clicking the Bullets button will create a bullet. The Increase and Decrease Paragraph Spacing buttons help you in modifying the spacing between bulleted items. The Promote and Demote buttons can move a bullet up or down a level.

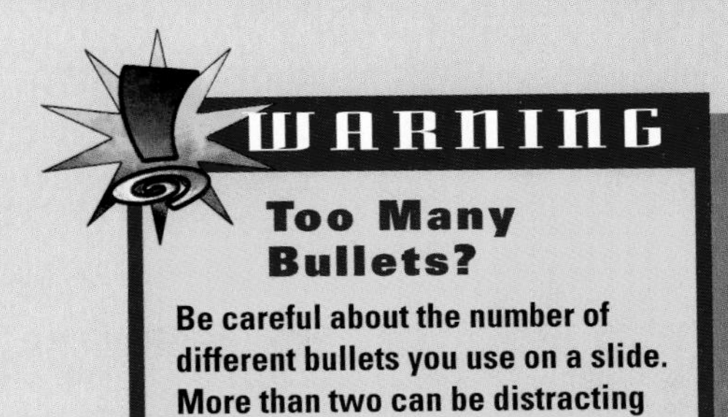

WARNING

Too Many Bullets?

Be careful about the number of different bullets you use on a slide. More than two can be distracting to viewers.

Printing a Presentation

PowerPoint provides different ways to print the contents of your presentation. In this lesson, you will print the presentation as a handout, which is typically used to hand out to your audience.

1. Select **File, Print** in the menu.
2. In the Print dialog box, click the **Print what drop-down arrow** and select **Handouts** and **6 slides per page** so that your entire presentation will print on a single sheet.
3. Notice in Figure 2.28 the default settings are set for Print range and Number of copies. Leave those unchanged.
4. Click **OK**.

FIGURE 2.28
Print Dialog box

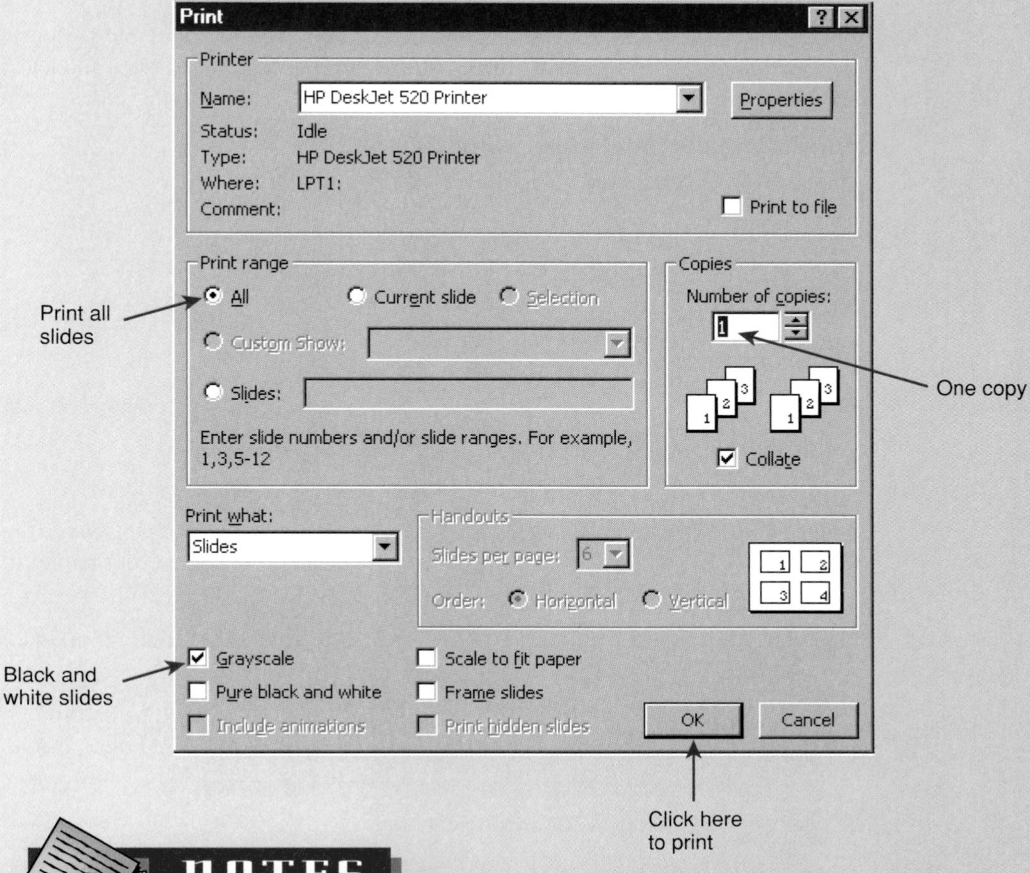

NOTES

Print Options

In the Print dialog box, you can select any of these check boxes to tailor your print job to the task.

Print to File	Send the output to a file instead of your printer
Collate	For more than one copy, collate your output (1, 2, 3, 1, 2, 3) rather than printing all copies of a page at one time (1, 1, 2, 2, 3, 3)
Pure Black and White	For black and white printers, this option prints out color slides more clearly.
Scale to Fit Paper	Compress slide to fit on a page.
Frame Slides	Print a border around each slide.
Print Hidden Slides	Print slides designated as hidden. (Doesn't appear when no slides are hidden.)

TIP

Stop Printing!

You can stop a print job you've started by double-clicking the printer icon displayed on the status bar when a print job is active. A red X appears over the icon and PowerPoint stops the printing.

STRENGTHENING YOUR SKILLS

1. You have been asked to create a training session on PowerPoint. **Open** the presentation **chap2-1**. Select **File, Save As** to save the file as PowerPoint Features and leave the original file unchanged. You will make a number of changes to the slides.
   - **a.** In **Slide Sorter view**, move slide 3 to slide 2.
   - **b.** In **Outline view**, do the following:
     - **i.** Collapse slides. Move slide 5 to slide 4.
     - **ii.** Expand the slide titles.
     - **iii.** Edit the title slide to include these words: *Beyond the Basics.* Replace the current name with your own as the author of this representation.
     - **iv.** Move the bulleted item Browse Web documents to the top of the list on that slide.
     - **v.** Demote the last two bulleted items in the Multimedia slide.
   - **c.** Go to **Slide view**, select the title, and change the font to Arial, 40 pt. Change the text color to red, and add bold and shadow. Change the subtitle (your name) to Arial, 28 pt., and make the text bold.
   - **d.** Go back to **Slide Sorter view** and delete slide 3 titled *Getting Help with Presentations*.
   - **e.** Go to the **Master Slide** and change the bullet style of the first-level text to one of your choice. Use the ruler to create more space between the bullet and its text. The bullets for all your slides will be affected.
   - **f.** **Save** and **print** an outline of the presentation.
2. For a class assignment you are asked to **create a résumé** in the format of a PowerPoint presentation. Your résumé should include slides such as *Background*, *Work Experience*, *Hobbies*, and other topics you would normally include in a résumé. Select Pulse as the presentation design. All the background, text, and bullet colors and styles will be preset for you. **Save** your presentation and **print** as handouts (six per page).
3. The **AutoContent Wizard** provides predefined slides that you edit to meet your needs. Suppose your boss has asked you to develop screens introducing a speaker. You decide who the speaker will be and follow the guidelines below to help you create a presentation.
   - **a.** Select **File, New**. Pick the **General tab**. Double-click the AutoContent Wizard.
   - **b.** Select *Introducing and Thanking a Speaker* as the type of presentation.
   - **c.** Type your text in place of the sample text provided for you.
   - **d.** Run your presentation to preview. **Save** and **print** your presentation.

4. Create a slide show using the Design Template called *Blends*. Your title screen should have Chat Rooms as the title and your name and today's date as subtitles. Enter the content for the remaining slides as shown below.

   a. Slide 2

      Options (Title of slide 2)

      Asynchronous Sharing (first bulleted item)

      Email (sub-bullet)

      Newsgroups (sub-bullet)

      Synchronous Sharing (second bulleted item)

      Real-Time Chat (sub-bullet)

      Teleconference (sub-bullet)

   b. Slide 3

      How Valuable? (Title of slide 3)

      Encourages collaboration among students (first bulleted item)

      Gives students immediate feedback (second bulleted item)

      Provides a method for communicating outside the classroom (third bulleted item)

   c. Slide 4

      Downside of Chat Rooms (Title of slide 4)

      Teacher monitoring required to avoid cluttering (first bulleted item)

      Availability of students at specified times (second bulleted item)

      Speedy responses and more attentiveness required (third bulleted item)

5. You have created a presentation related to the Web. Some changes need to be made to the slides. Retrieve the file **Chap 2-2** on your student disk. **Save** your file as *The Law and the Internet.*

   a. Go to slide 2 and add a title: *Building A Web Site.*

   b. In the same slide, insert a two-line subtitle: *Maria Cordero, Evergreen College.*

   c. Change the font and font size for both.

   d. Use the **Spelling and Grammar** button to check for errors in the slides and make any necessary corrections.

   e. Go to slide 4. Change the font color for the entire second bulleted item to a bright red.

   f. Move slide 2 to slide 1.

   g. Go to the **Slide Master** and in the **Footer** area, type in *Web Conference '99.*

   h. Save your work. Print the presentation as handouts (select six slides to a page).

6. The AutoContent Wizard can guide you in creating a presentation.

   a. Under Presentation Type, click the **General button** and select **Generic**. Click on the **Next** button to proceed through the wizard. The title of your presentation should be: *How to Succeed in College.* At the end of the process, your screen should look like Figure 2.29.

   b. Click to the **Outline view** to see the slides in their entirety.

   c. Use the outline as a guide and create a presentation that addresses strategies for success in college.

   d. Apply a new design template to the presentation.

   e. Save your work and print the presentation as handouts.

FIGURE 2.29

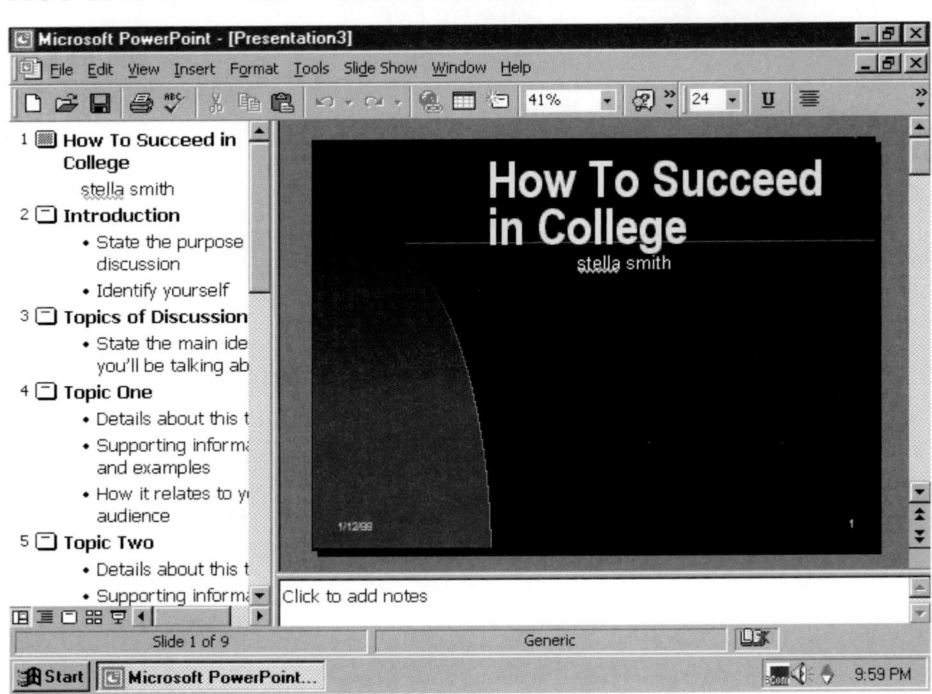

7. Select a chapter from your class textbook and create a PowerPoint presentation that clearly highlights the main topics and subtopics. Use your judgment as to how detailed the slides are, keeping in mind the design hints provided in this chapter.

8. Dale Carnegie & Associates has provided a number of templates to assist you in creating presentations. Since you have just been named President of Walden College, a small, liberal arts college in the South, you are grateful for this template. Under **File, New** in the menu, click the **Presentation** tab. Select *Managing Organizational Change,* a template created by Dale Carnegie and Associates. Use the template to create your presentation. Print the resulting outline.

SUMMARY OF FUNCTIONS

Task	Mouse/Button	Menu	Keyboard
Adding bold	Click the Bold button	Format, Font	[Ctrl] B
Bullets:			
Changing bullet style		Format, Bullets	[Alt] O B
Creating	Click the Bullets button		Enter
Deleting	Click the Bullets button		Backspace
Demoting	Click the Demote button		Tab
Promoting	Click the Promote button		[Shift] + Tab
Copying	Click the Copy button	Edit, Copy	[Ctrl] C
Cutting	Click the Cut button	Edit, Cut	[Ctrl] X
Creating a new presentation	Click the New button	File, New	[Ctrl] N
Finding	Click the Find button	Edit, Find	[Ctrl] F
Changing font color	Click the Font Color button	Format, Font	[Alt] O F
Changing font size	Click the Increase (Decrease) Font Size button	Format, Font	[Alt] O F
Outline:			
Expanding	Click the Expand button		[Alt] [Shift] +
Collapsing	Click the Collapse button		[Alt] [Shift] –
Moving up	Click the Move up button		[Alt] [Shift] Up Arrow
Moving down	Click the Move down button		[Alt] [Shift] Down Arrow
Pasting	Click the Paste button	Edit, Paste	[Ctrl] V
Printing	Click the Print button	File, Print	[Ctrl] P
Redoing	Click the Redo button	Edit, Redo	[Ctrl] Y
Replacing	Edit, Replace		[Ctrl] H
Adding shadow	Click the Shadow button	Format, Font	
Using the Slide Master	View, Master, Slide Master		[Alt] V M S
Using tools:			
AutoCorrect	Tools, AutoCorrect		[Alt] T A

Spelling checker	Click the Spell button	Tools, Spelling	F7
Style Checker	Tools, Options, Spelling & Style		[Alt] T O
Underlining	Click the Underline button	Format, Font	[Ctrl] U
Undoing	Click the Undo button	Edit, Undo	[Ctrl] Z

SELF-TEST PROBLEMS

True/False

Circle T for statements that are true and F for statements that are false.

T F **1.** The only tool for correcting text is the spell checker.

T F **2.** The AutoContent Wizard provides the most help in creating slides.

T F **3.** AutoCorrect settings are set by PowerPoint and cannot be added to.

T F **4.** The PowerPoint dialog box is available only when you first start PowerPoint.

T F **5.** PowerPoint provides 10 Autolayouts with various placeholders to create slides.

T F **6.** The Template provides the least amount of help in creating slides.

T F **7.** Pressing the Backspace key will delete a bullet.

T F **8.** Drag and drop works best in Slide view to move slides.

T F **9.** Collapsing and expanding slide titles is a feature unique to the Slide Sorter view.

T F **10.** The Promote button on the Drawing toolbar moves text up a level.

Multiple Choice

Select the best answer for each question and write the corresponding letter in the blank.

_______ **1.** Which steps result in moving text?
- **a.** Select the text to be moved, press Ctrl + C
- **b.** Select the text, click Edit, Cut in the menu
- **c.** Both (a) and (b)
- **d.** Neither (a) nor (b)

_______ **2.** Which is the first step in entering text in Slide view?
- **a.** Type in new text
- **b.** Click anywhere in a new slide and enter new text
- **c.** Click in the placeholder box to position the insertion point before typing
- **d.** None of the above

_______ **3.** Which of the following commands are used to create a new presentation?
- **a.** File, New
- **b.** File, Open
- **c.** View, Slide
- **d.** Format, Apply Design

_______ **4.** Which of the following can be changed after inserting a slide?
- **a.** Its location in the presentation
- **b.** Its layout
- **c.** Both of the above
- **d.** None of the above

_______ **5.** While in Outline view, which of the following is true?
- **a.** A black-and-white slide of the first slide in a presentation appears in miniature.
- **b.** A colored version of the current slide appears in miniature if you select View, Slide Miniature.
- **c.** A black-and-white slide of the current slide shows by default.
- **d.** None of the above.

_______ **6.** In which view is it possible to view the outline, screen and notes simultaneously?
- **a.** Normal View
- **b.** Slide Sorter
- **c.** Outline
- **d.** Slide

_______ **7.** To terminate a printing job, click the icon located on the
- **a.** Status bar
- **b.** Formatting toolbar
- **c.** Menu
- **d.** Draw toolbar

_______ **8.** To change a font for all slides
- **a.** Select Edit, Font in the menu
- **b.** Select Increase or Decrease Font Size buttons on the Formatting toolbar
- **c.** Select View, Master to edit Slide Master
- **d.** Select Format, Font in the menu

_______ **9.** After typing a line of text in Outline view and pressing the Enter key, where is the insertion point?
- **a.** At the next line, with a bullet appearing at the same level
- **b.** At the next blank line
- **c.** At the next line, with a bullet appearing at a lower level
- **d.** At the next line, with a bullet appearing at a higher level

_______ **10.** Design guidelines for creating screens include which of the following?
- **a.** Use color sparingly
- **b.** More than two bullet styles can be distracting
- **c.** Limit bullets to no more than three levels
- **d.** All of the above

Matching

Match each of the elements to the PowerPoint screen shown in the figure below with its resulting action.

FIGURE 2.30

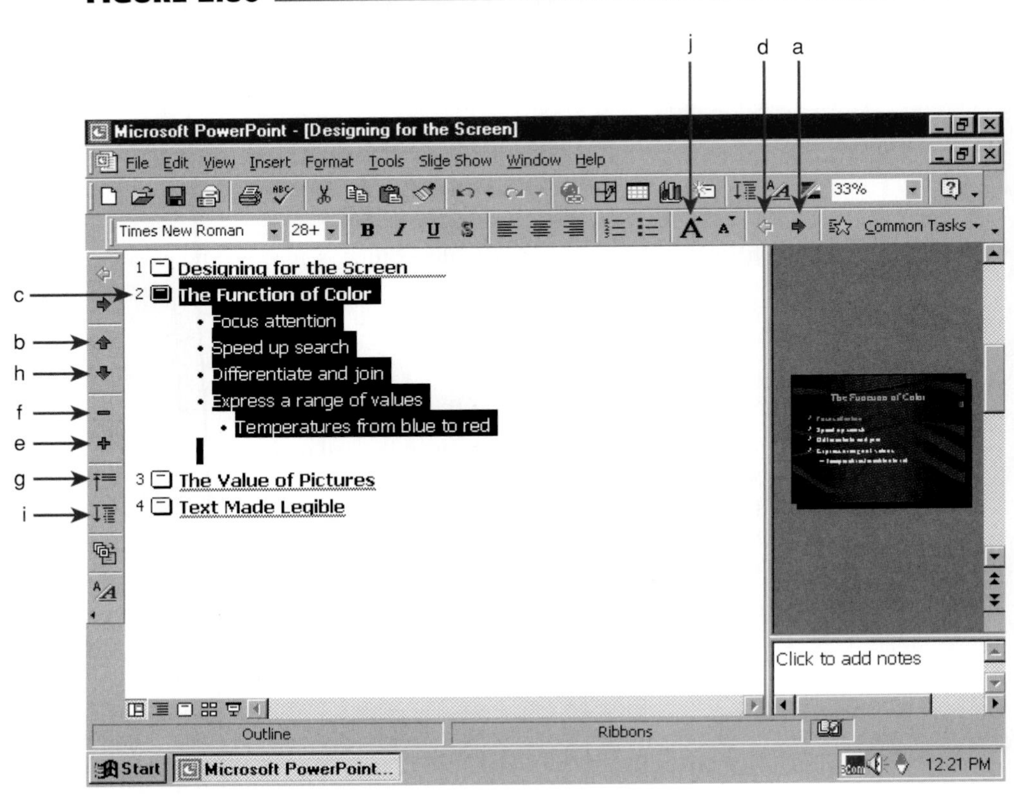

Click on	Action
______	**1.** Collapses all slides
______	**2.** Selects a slide
______	**3.** Expands a selected slide
______	**4.** Expands all slides
______	**5.** Moves up an item
______	**6.** Promotes a bullet
______	**7.** Demotes a bullet
______	**8.** Increases font size
______	**9.** Moves down an item
______	**10.** Collapses a slide

Fill in the Blank

Fill in the blank with the missing word or phrase.

1. To print material to give to an audience, the best printing option to select is __________.
2. To create a new presentation, select _______ ______ in the menu.

3. When collapsed titles appear on a screen, a ____ _____ appears to indicate there are more items that are not appearing.
4. The ___________ button can be used to print an existing presentation or the ________ ________ menu selections can be used to print.
5. In Outline view with slides collapsed, press the _____ ______ button to change the position of the selected slide so that slide 4 would become slide 3.
6. A wavy red line indicates a _____ error.
7. The ____ menu choice contains the Undo command.
8. When in Slide view, clicking the ____ button on the Standard toolbar leaves a thin line where a slide was located.
9. The _____ toolbar contains the button that changes text color.
10. The ___ ____ appears on the screen to show alternate views of a slide.

ANSWERS

True/False: 1. F 2. T 3. F 4. T 5. F 6. F 7. T 8. F 9. F 10. F

Multiple Choice: 1. b 2. c 3. a 4. d 5. b 6. a 7. a 8. c 9. a 10. d

Matching: 1. g 2. c 3. e 4. i 5. b 6. d 7. a 8. j 9. h 10. f

Fill in the Blank: 1. Handouts 2. File, New 3. gray line 4. Print; File, Print 5. Move up 6. spelling 7. Edit 8. Cut 9. Drawing 10. Color slide

Enhancing a Presentation

OUTLINE

Creating a Data Chart
Changing Chart Appearance
Importing an Excel File
Creating a Table
Editing a Table
Creating an Organization Chart
Adding Clip Art
Using Drawing Tools
Creating WordArt Text
Strengthening Your Skills
Summary of Functions
Self-Test Problems and Answers

LEARNING OBJECTIVES

After completing this chapter, you will be able to:

- Create and edit a data chart
- Import an Excel file
- Create and edit a table
- Create an organization chart
- Add clip art
- Apply WordArt to text
- Use Drawing tools

Creating a Data Chart

Creating a chart to display information provides a more visually appealing method to communicate with your audience. In this section, you will create a chart displaying sales figures for Buy and Save Shoes, Inc.

1. Select **File, New** in the menu. The PowerPoint dialog box appears.
2. Click the **General tab, Blank Presentation, OK**.
3. Click the **AutoLayout** for a **chart**. (The AutoLayout at the end of row 2.)
4. Double-click the **chart placeholder** to add a chart.
5. The data displayed in the table (or datasheet) is for demonstration only (Figure 3.1). Click in the cell where East is displayed and replace with **Barrow**. Press the **right arrow** (or click with your mouse) to move to the next cell. Type in the remaining data as shown in Figure 3.2.

(continued on page 94)

FIGURE 3.1
The Datasheet

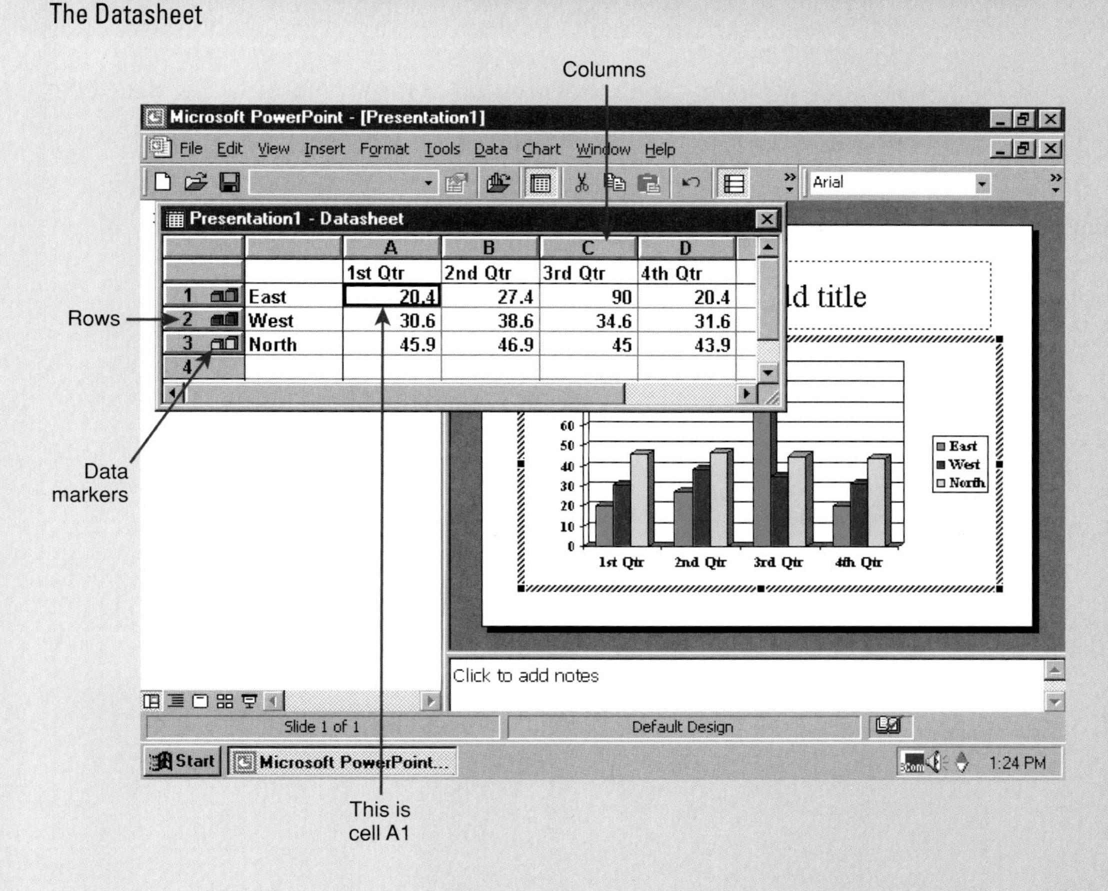

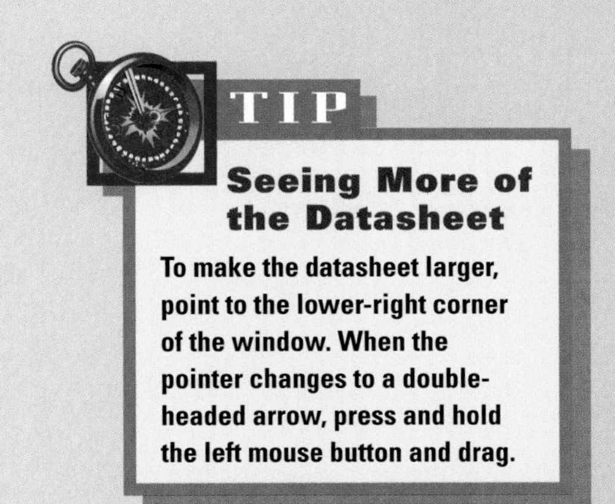

TIP

Seeing More of the Datasheet

To make the datasheet larger, point to the lower-right corner of the window. When the pointer changes to a double-headed arrow, press and hold the left mouse button and drag.

Creating a Data Chart (continued)

6. Click the **View, Datasheet button** to turn it off. Now the datasheet is removed and you can see your chart.
7. Type **East Region Sales** in the Title placeholder.
8. **Save** your file to wherever your student files are stored. Name your file **Sales Projections**.

FIGURE 3.2
Quarterly Sales Figures–East Region

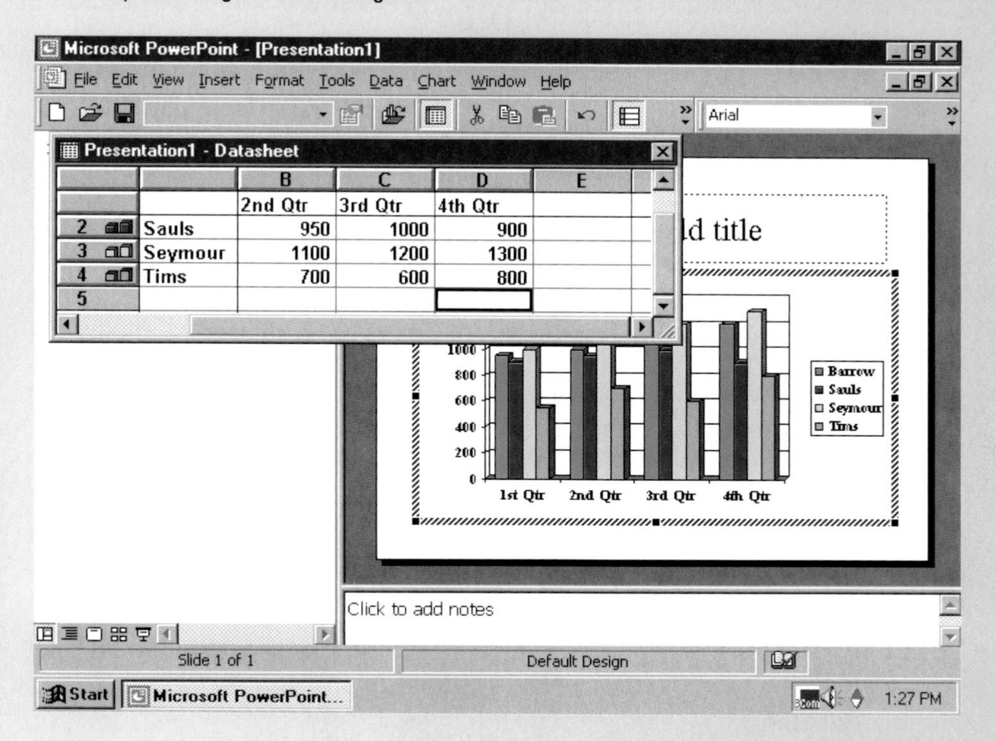

NOTES

Chart Talk

Data are displayed in two views: either as a **datasheet** or as a **chart**. The datasheet is made up of **cells**, which store your data. A **cell address** indicates the location of data. For example, cell address A1 represents column A row 1. A group of data from a row or column is defined as a **data series**. The chart displays a data series in a unique color or pattern. **Data markers** are the symbols, such as bars, lines, or pie slices, used to display data.

Changing Chart Appearance

If you are not in the file Sales Projections that you began in the previous lesson, open the file. In this lesson, you will edit your chart.

1 Double-click the chart to **open** it. A thatched border appears around the chart. Click the **View, Datasheet** to display the datasheet.

2 **Select the range** of cells containing the sales figures. The active cell has a thick border and the other cells are shaded in black.

3 Select **Format** and then **Number** in the **Menu**. Select **Currency** and set the decimals to **0** as shown in Figure 3.3. Click **OK**.

4 To change data in your chart, simply click in the cell. For instance, click in the cell for Tims, 4th Qtr and change 800 to 900. Click outside the box or press ENTER. The chart under the datasheet adjusts to the change.

5 By default, charts are displayed as columns. To change, click the arrow next to the **Chart Type button** on the Standard toolbar. Click **Bar Chart**.

6 To add text to the Y axis label, select **Chart, Chart Options**. Click the **Titles tab**.

(continued on page 98)

FIGURE 3.3
Edited Datasheet

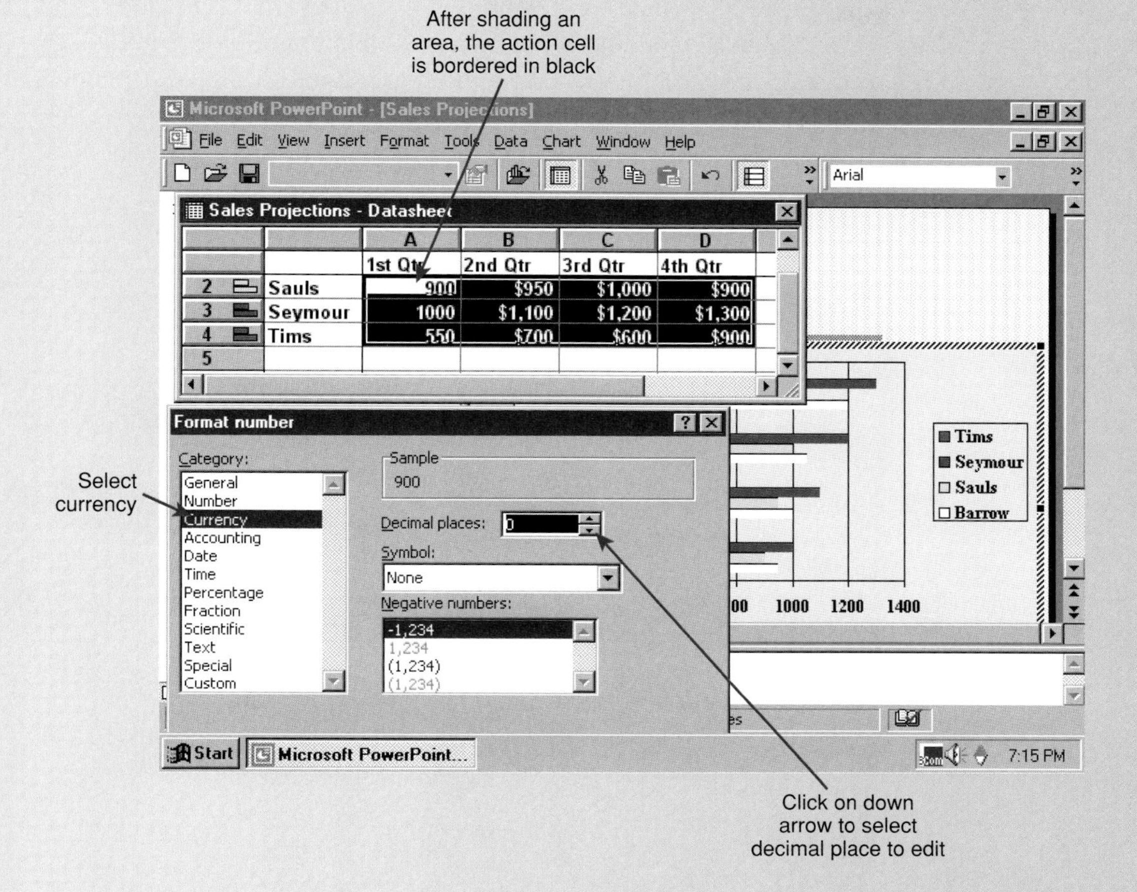

TIP

Changing Text Appearance

Just as in a word processing document, you can change fonts, font styles, and font size. Either selecting Format in the menu to view the options or typing formatting in Help will give you a wide range of choices for changing text appearance.

Changing Chart Appearance (continued)

7 In the **Value Y axis box**, type: **(in thousands of dollars)** to add text to the Y axis label. Click **OK**. Your chart should look like the one shown in Figure 3.4.

8 **Save** your work.

FIGURE 3.4
Edited Chart

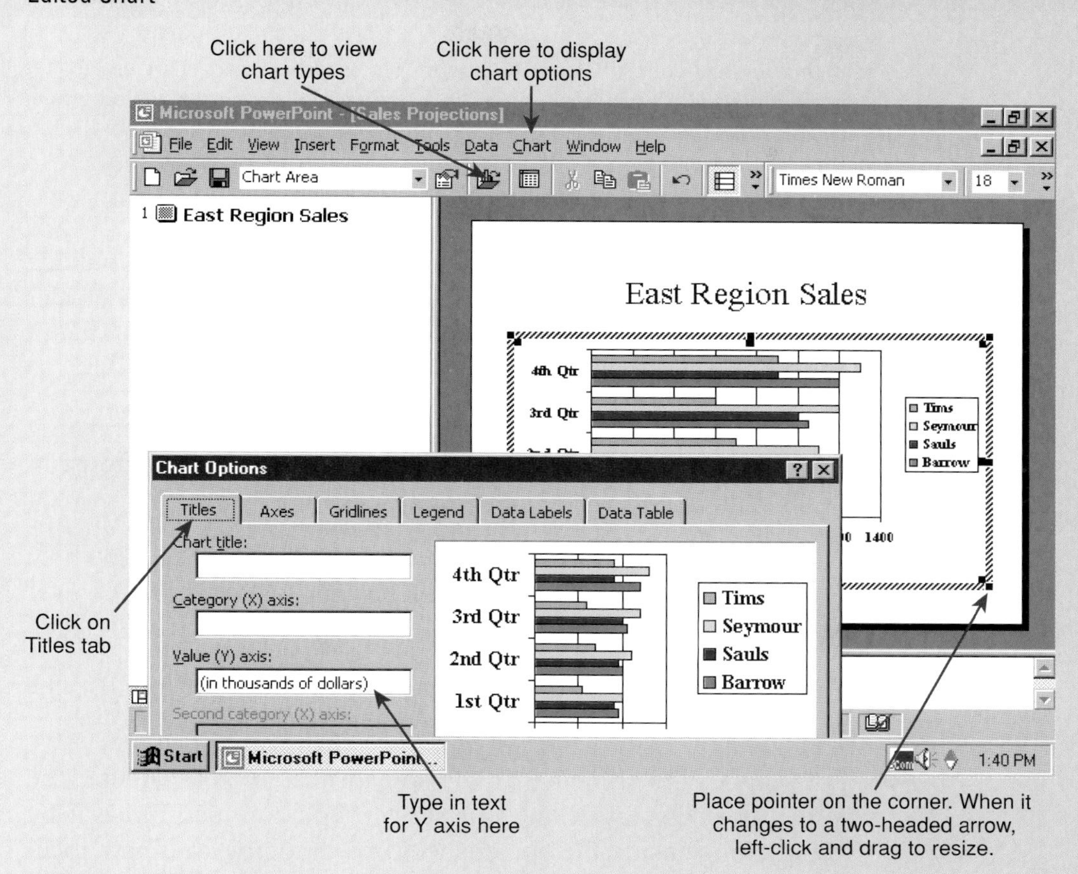

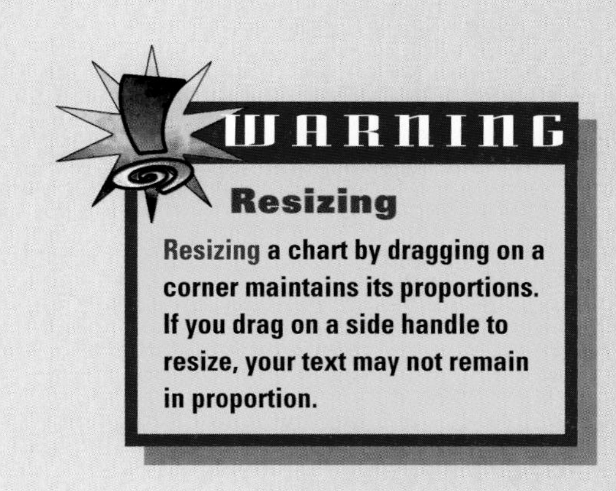

Importing an Excel File

In this lesson, you will learn to import a spreadsheet and chart created in Excel, a powerful spreadsheet program. Microsoft has integrated the programs in Office to allow this easy process of sharing information.

1. Make sure the **Sales Projections** file in PowerPoint is open.
2. If the chart has been selected for editing, click anywhere outside the chart to deselect it. (You should not see the thatched border around the chart.) Select **Insert, New Slide** and click the **Object AutoLayout** (the last item in the fourth row).
3. Double-click the **Object placeholder**. In the Insert Object dialog box, scroll in the **Object Type list box** and highlight **Microsoft Excel Worksheet**.
4. Click **Create from File**. Click the **Browse button** as shown in Figure 3.5. In the **Look in box**, select your **a:\ drive** or wherever your student files are stored. Click **Total Sales by Region**.
5. Click **OK** to close the **Browse dialog box**. Click **OK** to close the **Insert Object dialog box**.
6. The handles are showing on the spreadsheet so you can size the spreadsheet displayed on your screen. You can also move it by left-clicking inside the spreadsheet and dragging to a new location.
7. Click in the **Title placeholder** and type **Buy and Save Shoes**. Compare your screen to Figure 3.6.
8. **Save** your work.

FIGURE 3.5
Insert Object Dialog Box

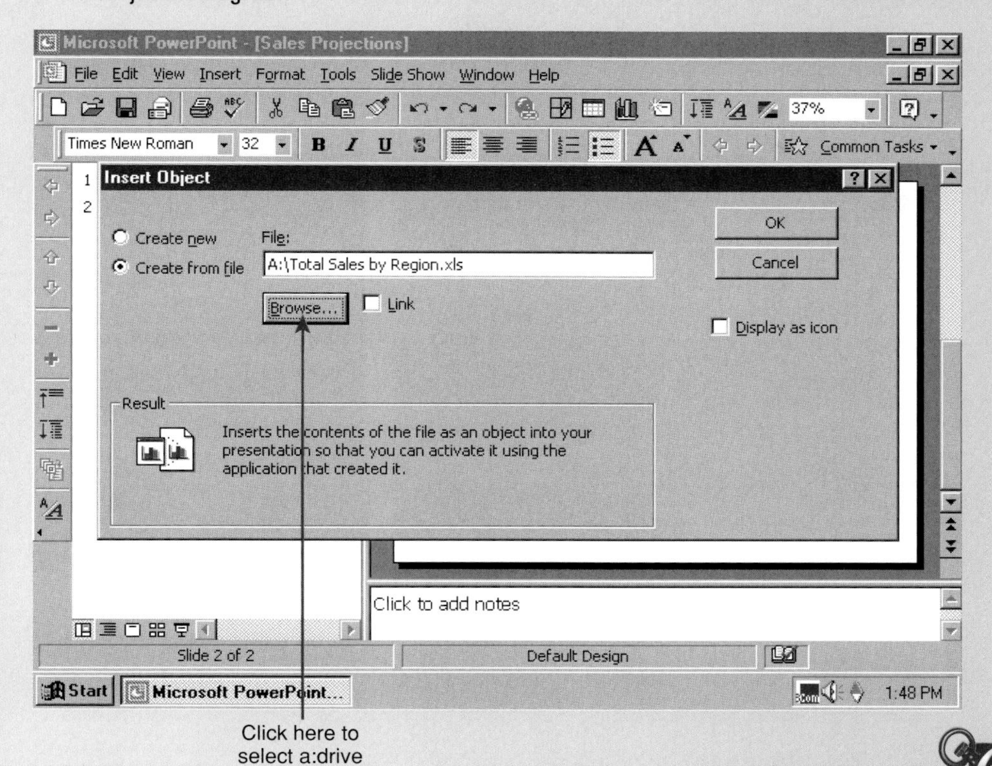

FIGURE 3.6
Imported Excel File

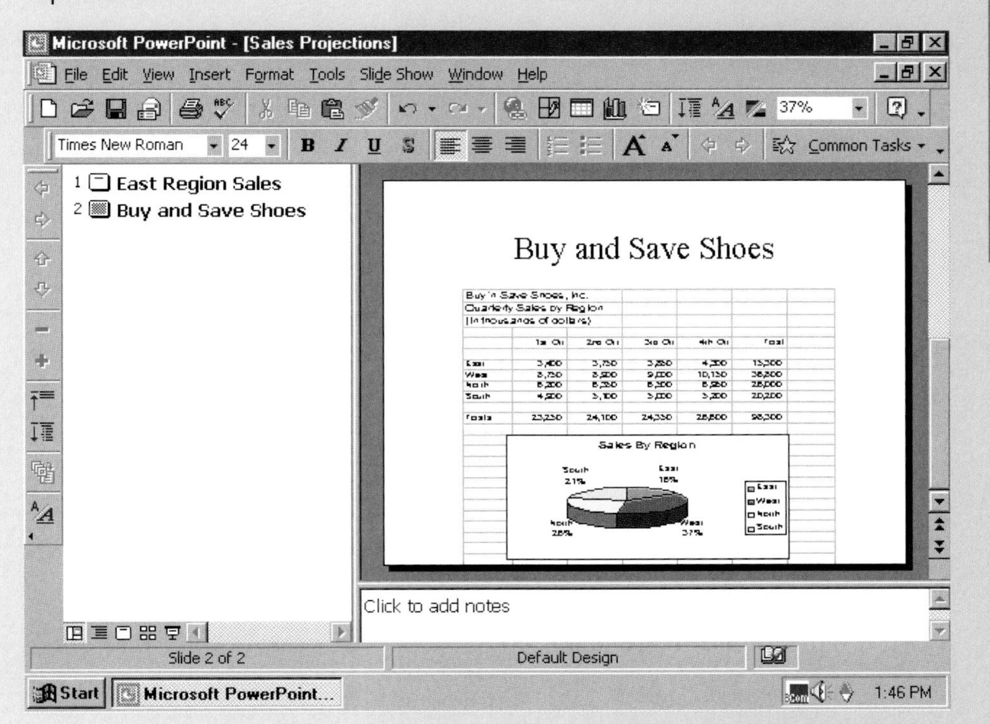

TIP

Editing in Excel

You can double-click an Excel worksheet to make editing changes. Although you remain in PowerPoint, the toolbars and menus relate to Excel tasks.

Creating a Table

In the following steps, you will learn how to create a table in PowerPoint. Tables are composed of columns and rows for entering data. To create a table, you will use Microsoft Word toolbars and commands.

1. If you are not in the **Sales Projections** file, **open** the file now.
2. Let's select a template for this presentation. Select **Format, Apply Design Template** to display a list of the various templates. Click **Bold Stripes**. Click **Apply**.
3. Go to **slide 2** and click the **New Slide button** to add another slide to the presentation.
4. Click the **AutoLayout** for **Title Only** (third row, third from the left). Click OK.
5. Click in the **Title placeholder** and type **Shoe Styles.**
6. Select **Insert, Picture, Microsoft Word Table** in the menu. In Number of columns, **type 2**. In Number of rows, **type 4** as shown in Figure 3.7. Click **OK**. The **Word table** appears on your slide.

(continued on page 104)

FIGURE 3.7
The Table Grid

Microsoft PowerPoint - [Sales Projections]

File Edit View Insert Format Tools Slide Show Window Help

1 East Region Sales
2 Buy and Save Shoes
3 Shoe Styles

Shoe Styles

Insert Table

Number of columns: 2

Number of rows: 4

OK

Cancel

Click to add notes

Slide 3 of 3 | Bold Stripes

Start | Microsoft PowerPoint... | 2:33 PM

Enter number of columns here

Click OK to exit

Enter number of rows here

Tables Everywhere!

You can use Microsoft Office Word, Excel or Access to create tables. For complex graphics formatting such as bulleted lists and custom tabs, use Word. For complex calculations and charts, use Excel. For a table used in a presentation, use PowerPoint.

NOTES

What Is Embedding?

When you embed an object, you actually open one program inside of another. In these tutorials, this was done twice: first, with the Excel spreadsheet and now with the Word table. Both these objects are edited inside their respective programs.

Creating a Table (continued)

7. **Enter** the information into your table as shown in Figure 3.8. Press **Tab** to move from one cell to the next. Press **Shift + Tab** to move backward.

8. After entering the data, click anywhere outside the table. **Save** your work. Remain in this file to edit the table in the next lesson.

FIGURE 3.8
Table with Information

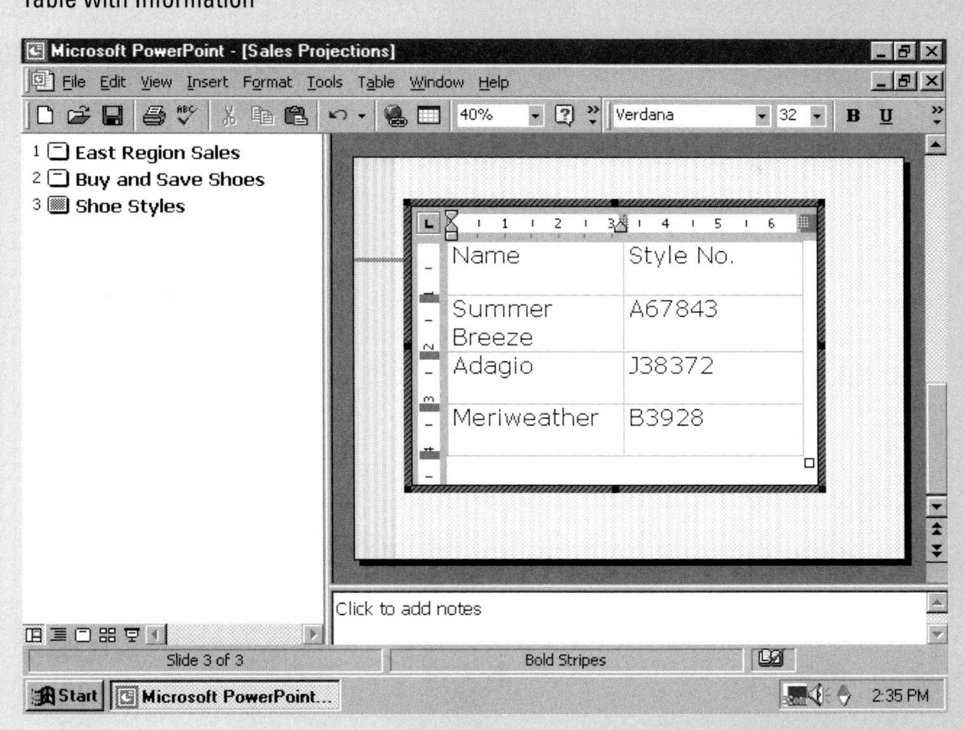

Changing Templates

You can apply a new template to a presentation even if you have already selected a template. Select Format in the menu and click Apply Design Template to change a template design.

Editing a Table

You can change your table appearance by inserting a column, changing text, and moving the table.

1. At **slide 3** in your presentation, move your pointer anywhere inside the table area on your slide. When the pointer changes to a four-headed arrow, left-click and drag to **move** the table so it is placed further below the title.
2. **Double-click** the table to open it for editing. **To insert a column between Name and Style No.**, position the pointer in the ruler above the Name column to the right of where you want the new column.
3. When the pointer changes to a downward-pointing arrow, click to select the column (Figure 3.9). Right-click and select **Insert Columns** on the **Shortcut menu**.

(continued on page 108)

FIGURE 3.9
Column Selected for Insertion

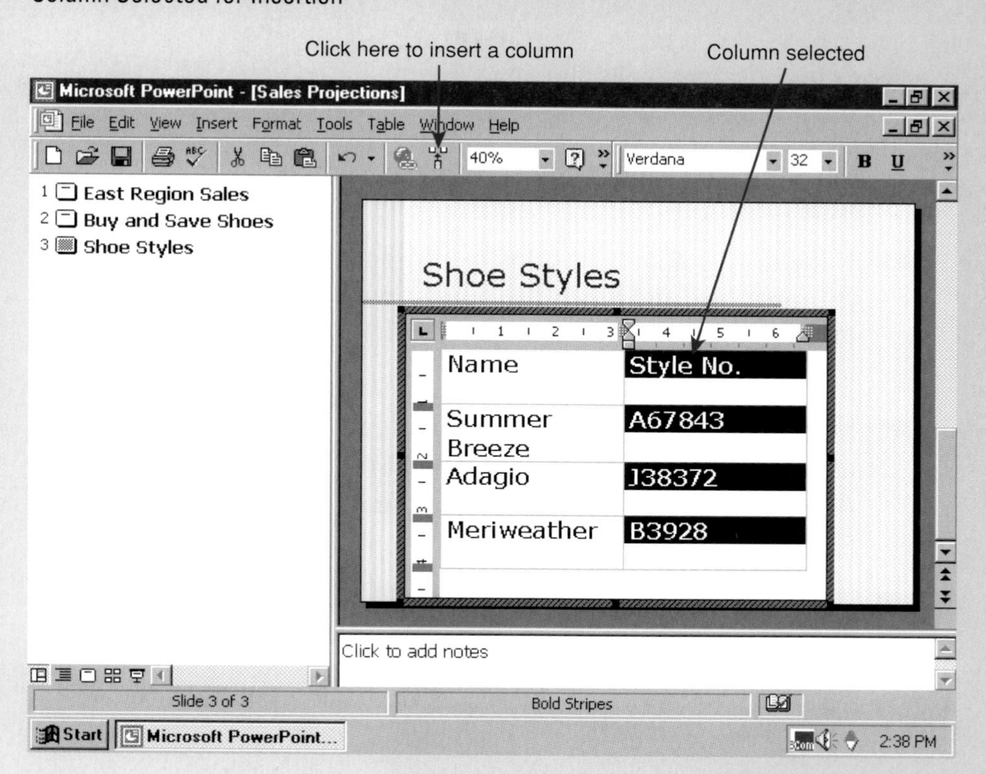

TIP

Finding the Black Arrow

When inserting a column, it may be difficult to locate the black arrow. Move your pointer around above the column and close to the ruler and it will appear.

Editing a Table (continued)

4. **Enter** information as shown in Figure 3.10.

5. While still in editing mode, click the heading **Name** and then click the **Underline button**. **Repeat** for the remaining two headings.

6. If the third column does not show, go to the upper-right corner of the table box and when the pointer changes to a **double-headed arrow**, click and drag until the third column is displayed. Click anywhere outside the table.

7. Select the title of the slide by clicking the flashing insertion point and dragging it across the title **Shoe Styles**. Then click the **Center Alignment button**. Compare your screen to the one in Figure 3.10.

8. To adjust column widths, take your pointer to the border separating a column. When the pointer changes to a black, two-headed arrow, click and drag to resize the column.

9. **Save** your work.

FIGURE 3.10
Finished Table

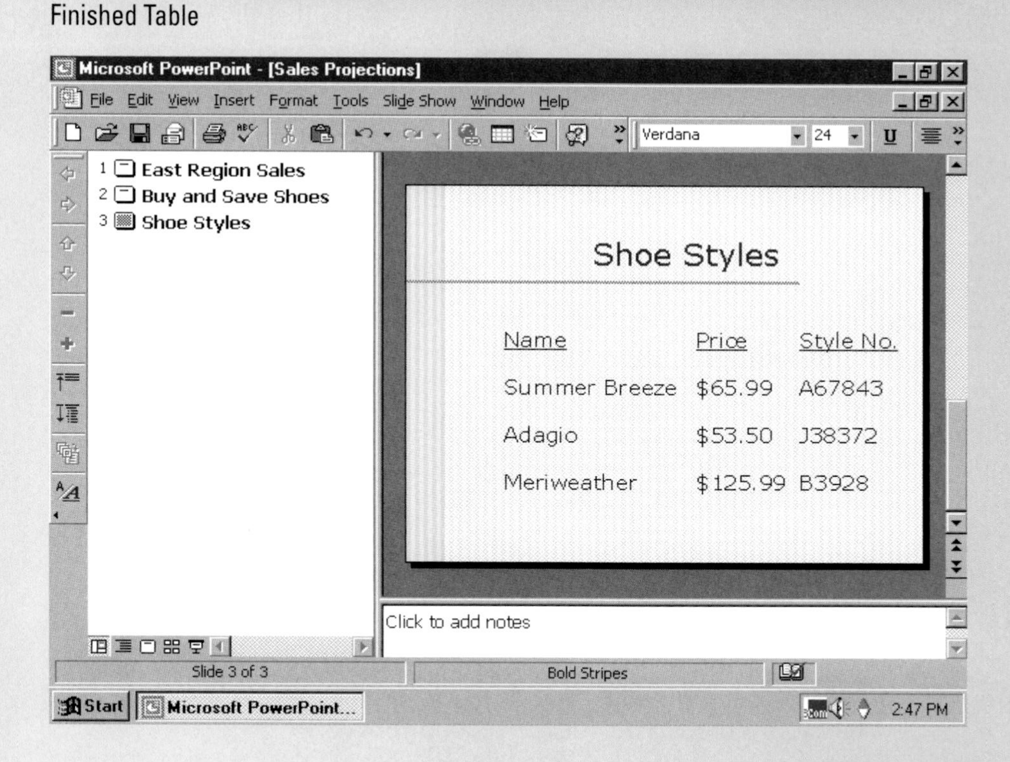

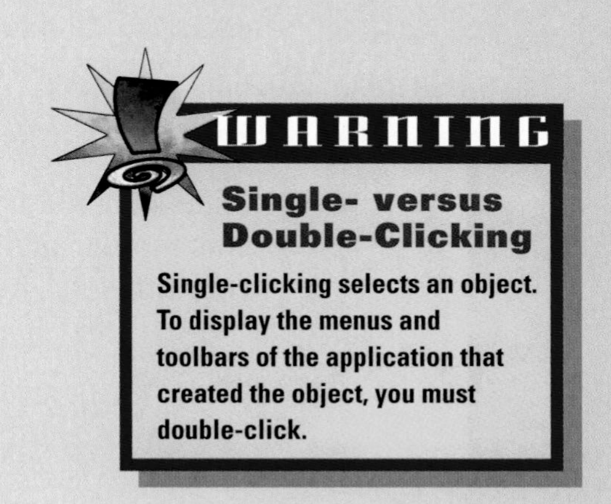

Single- versus Double-Clicking

Single-clicking selects an object. To display the menus and toolbars of the application that created the object, you must double-click.

Creating an Organization Chart

An organization chart is an effective way to visually show reporting relationships in an organization. In this lesson, you will create an organization chart for Buy and Save Shoes, Inc.

1. If you are not in the **Sales Projections** file, **open** the file now. Go to **slide 3** and click the **New Slide button**.
2. In the **New Slide dialog box**, choose the **Organization Chart AutoLayout** (second row, third from left).
3. Double-click the **placeholder** to add the organization chart.
4. You should see the **Microsoft Organization Chart window** on your screen as shown in Figure 3.11. Click the **Maximize button** of this window.
5. The text of the first box is already selected. Type **Rosemary Preston**. Press **Enter**. Type **President** for her title.
6. Click in the **first box** of the second row. Enter the information as shown in Figure 3.12 for the second row.
7. Click the **Subordinate button** on the Organization Chart toolbar. Then click in the **Marketing & Sales box** to add the first two subordinates. Repeat to add two more subordinates.
8. In the first subordinate box, type **Janet Newton**. Press **Enter**. Type **East Sales Mgr.** Check Figure 3.12 for names to add in other subordinate boxes.
9. Select **File** in the menu. Click **Exit and Return to Sales Projections**. Click **Yes** when asked whether to update the object.
10. Slide 4 should now display an organization chart. Click the **Title placeholder** and type the title as shown in Figure 3.12. **Center** your title. **Save** your work.

FIGURE 3.11
Placeholders for the Organization Chart

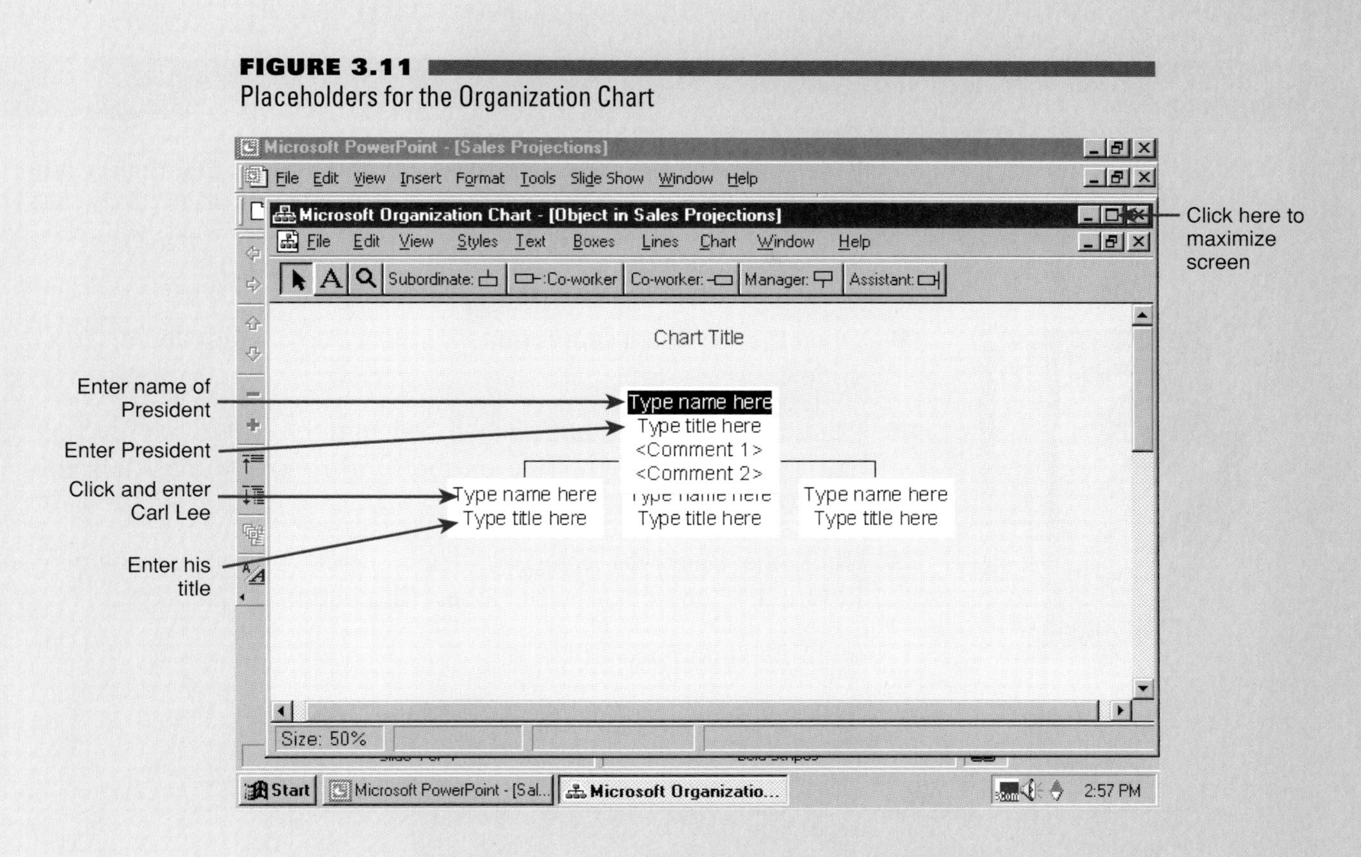

FIGURE 3.12
Completed Organization Chart

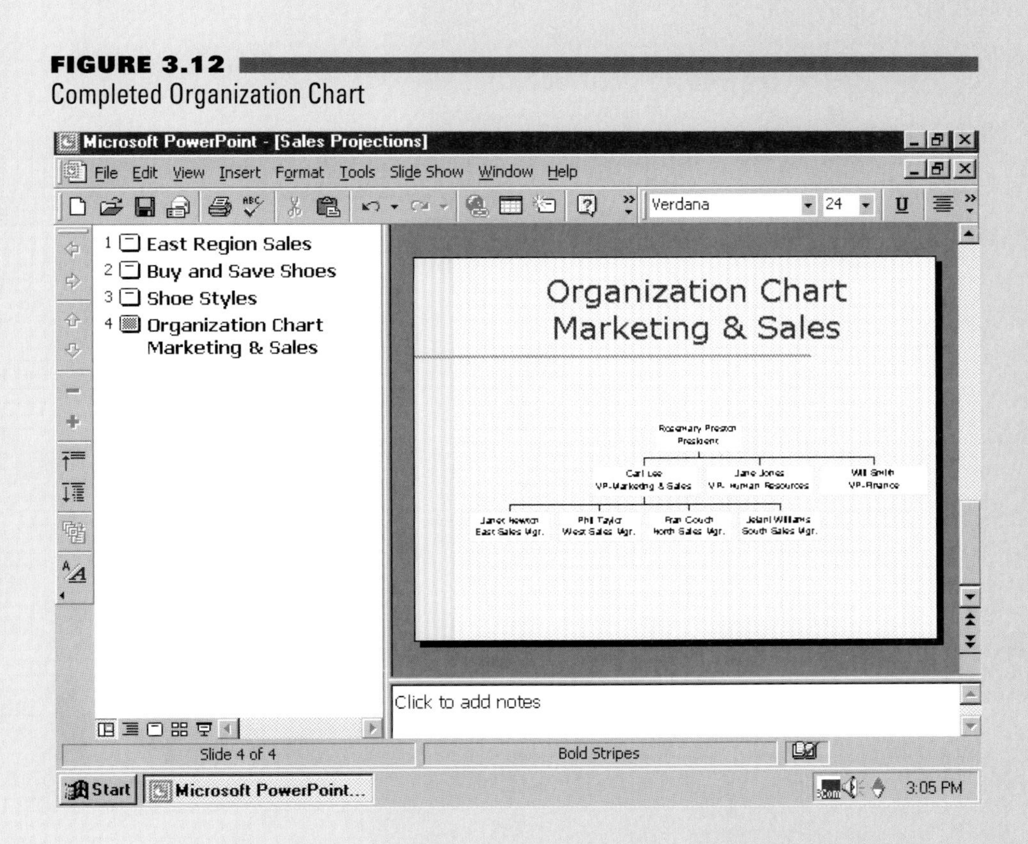

Adding Clip Art

PowerPoint provides a selection of electronic clip art in its **Clip Gallery** that you can use to spark interest in your presentation. Pictures can effectively convey a message or a tone to a presentation. In the steps below you will create another slide using **clip art**.

1. Open the file **Sales Projections** if you are not already there. Go to **slide 4**.
2. Click the **New Slide button**. Select the AutoLayout for Text and Clip Art (the first slide on the third row). Double-click the **Clip Art placeholder**.
3. Click the **Business** category. Then select the image shown in Figure 3.13 and click on the **Insert Clip button**.

(continued on page 114)

FIGURE 3.13
Microsoft Clip Gallery

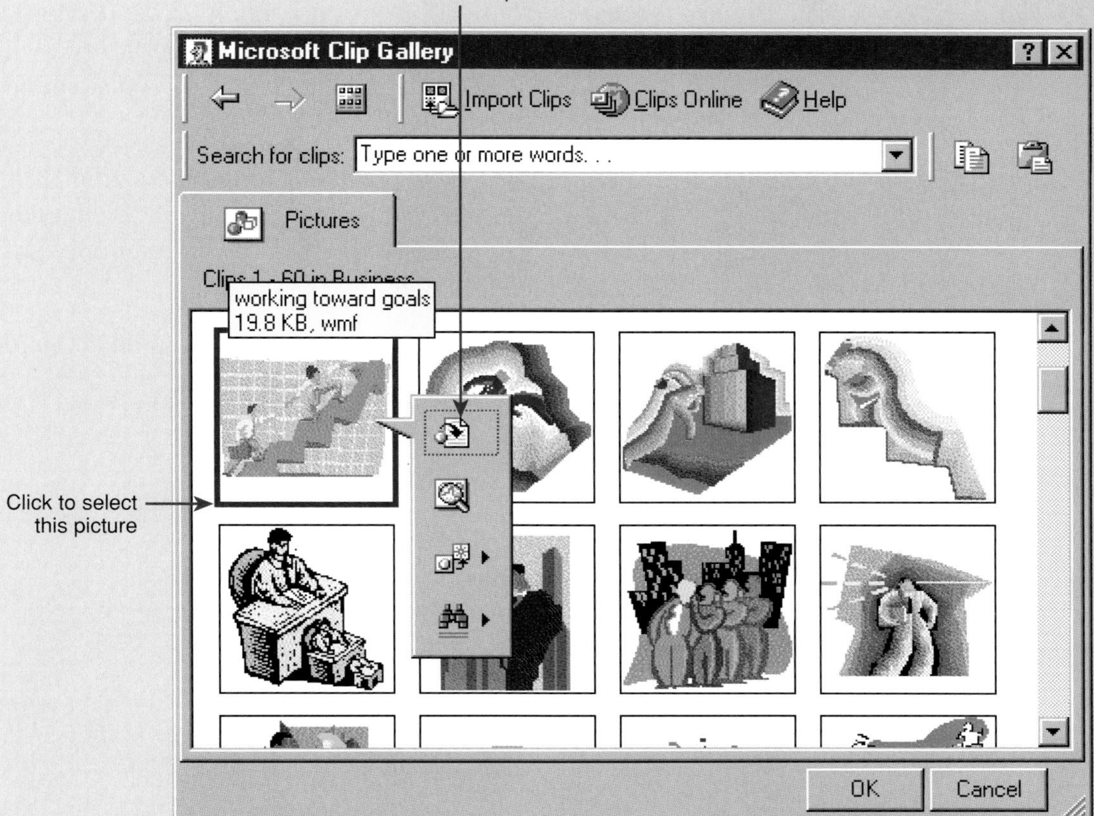

NOTES

Clip Gallery on the Web

The new Clip Gallery provides you with more pictures, sounds and motion clips. You can access additional clip art if you have a Web connection. From the Office Clip Gallery, click the Clips Online button. This will connect you to Clip Gallery Live, a Web site where you can preview additional clips.

Adding Clip Art (continued)

4. The **Picture toolbar** pops up. (If it does not, click View, Toolbars, Picture.) Click the **Recolor Picture button**. Click the drop-down arrow as shown in Figure 3.14 and select red as the replacement color. This changes the tie color. Click **OK**.

5. Click the image on your slide to select it. Notice the sizing handles appear. Go to one of the corners. When your pointer changes to a two-headed black arrow, **click and drag** your pointer outward to resize your picture so it is larger.

6. Refer to Figure 3.15 for text added to the slide. Select the text and click the **Bold button** B.

7. **Save** your work.

FIGURE 3.14
Recoloring Picture

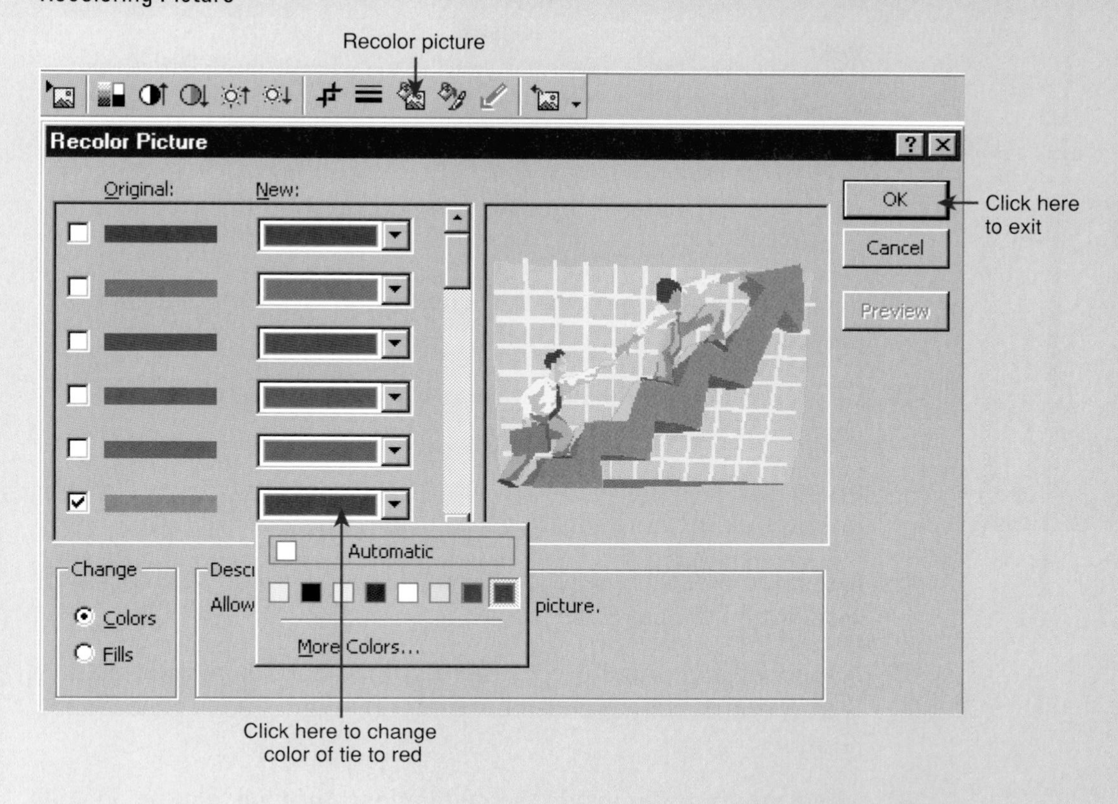

FIGURE 3.15
Clip Art Displayed on Slide

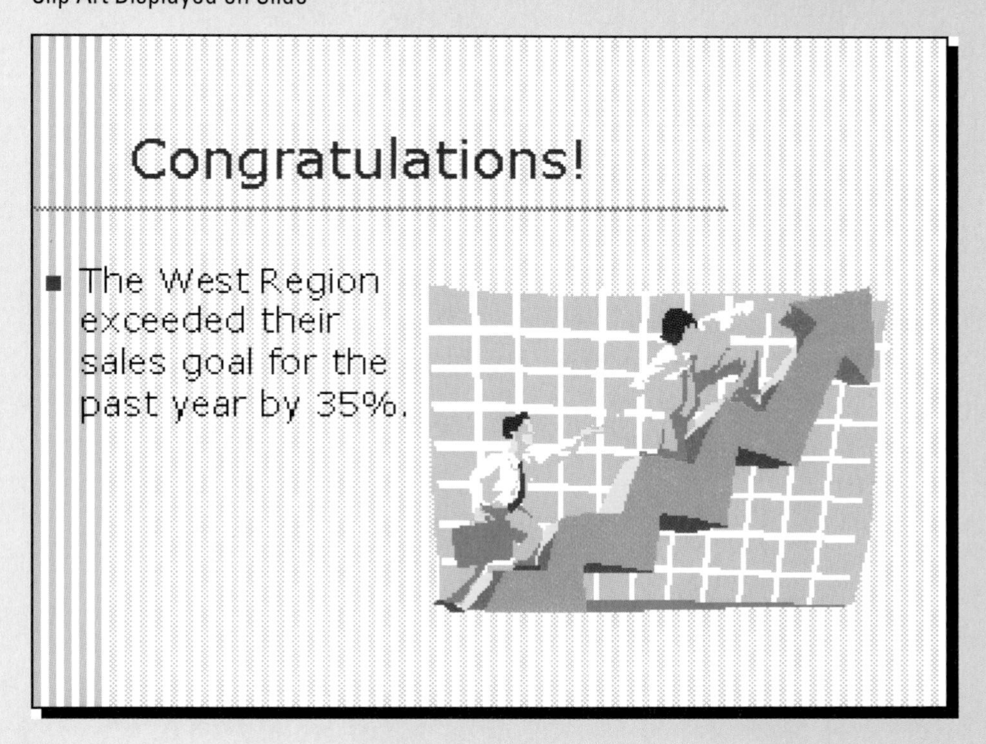

Using Drawing Tools

PowerPoint provides a variety of drawing tools to enhance your screen images. In the steps below you will use the Drawing toolbar to create a message on a previously created slide.

1. Open the file **Sales Projections** if you are not already there. Go to **slide 2**.
2. Select **View** in the menu and click **Ruler** if the ruler is not displayed.
3. Click the **Rectangle tool** on the **Drawing toolbar**. Your pointer changes to a crosshair.
4. Move the crosshair around the screen and notice the moving markers on the horizontal and vertical rulers.
5. Move the crosshair until the vertical marker is at 0 and the horizontal marker is at $3^1/_2$.
6. Now click and drag the crosshair until the horizontal ruler marker is at 5 (on the edge) and the vertical marker is at 1. Release the pointer.
7. Move your pointer inside the rectangle, right-click and select **Add text**. Type **Last Year's**. Press **Enter**. Type **Leader**. Select the text and change the font size to **16** pt. Refer to Figure 3.16 for guidance.
8. Click the **Arrow tool** in the Drawing toolbar to select it. Again, your pointer changes to a crosshair. Position it to the left side of the rectangle.
9. Hold the **Shift key** and click your pointer at the same time and drag to the left, pointing to the location as shown in Figure 3.16. Release the pointer. An arrow appears.
10. If you need to reposition the arrow, place your pointer on the arrow. When it changes to a **four-headed arrow**, click and drag your pointer to move the arrow's location.
11. **Save** your work.

FIGURE 3.16
The Draw Tools

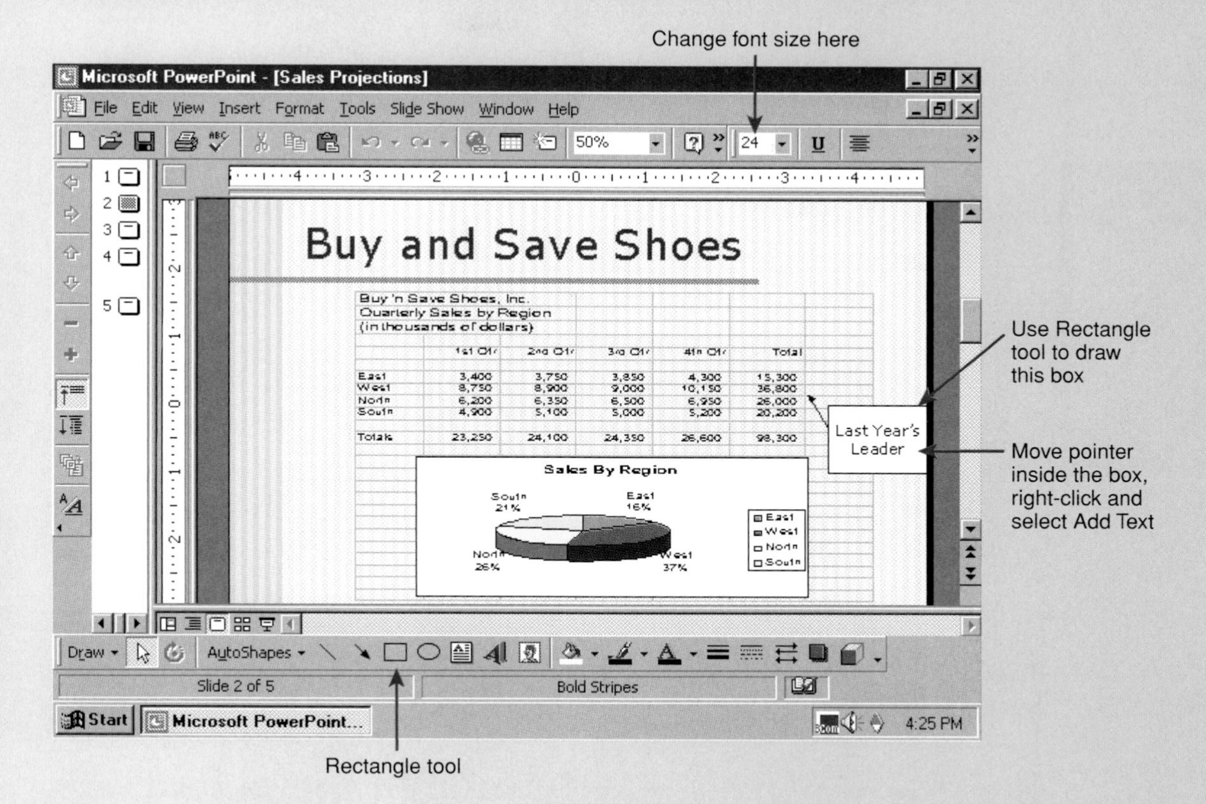

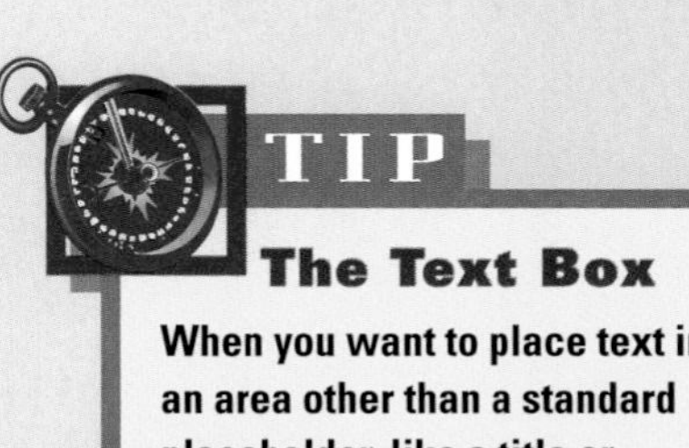

TIP

The Text Box

When you want to place text in an area other than a standard placeholder, like a title or bulleted list, you can create a text box. Use a text box to add text—such as captions—to pictures or graphics.

NOTES

AutoShapes Galore!

PowerPoint provides 6 new AutoShapes categories and more than 155 different AutoShapes, ranging from common shapes such as stars and hearts to atypical shapes related to Web sites and office layouts. The most common of these shapes, such as the rectangle and oval, reside directly on the Drawing toolbar. Once you select an AutoShape, you can resize, reshape, and fill it with the color of your choice.

Creating WordArt Text

WordArt lets you create stylized text to highlight your message. Because it displays in dramatic ways, it should be used sparingly.

1. Open the file **Sales Projections** if you are not already there. Go to **slide 5**.
2. Click the **New Slide button** . Select the AutoLayout for Blank (the last slide on the third row).
3. Click the **Insert WordArt button** on the **Drawing toolbar**.
4. In the **WordArt Gallery dialog box** (Figure 3.17), select the fifth format in the fourth row.
5. In the **Edit WordArt text box** (Figure 3.18), type **That's All Folks!** Click **OK**.

(continued on page 120)

FIGURE 3.17
Select WordArt Style

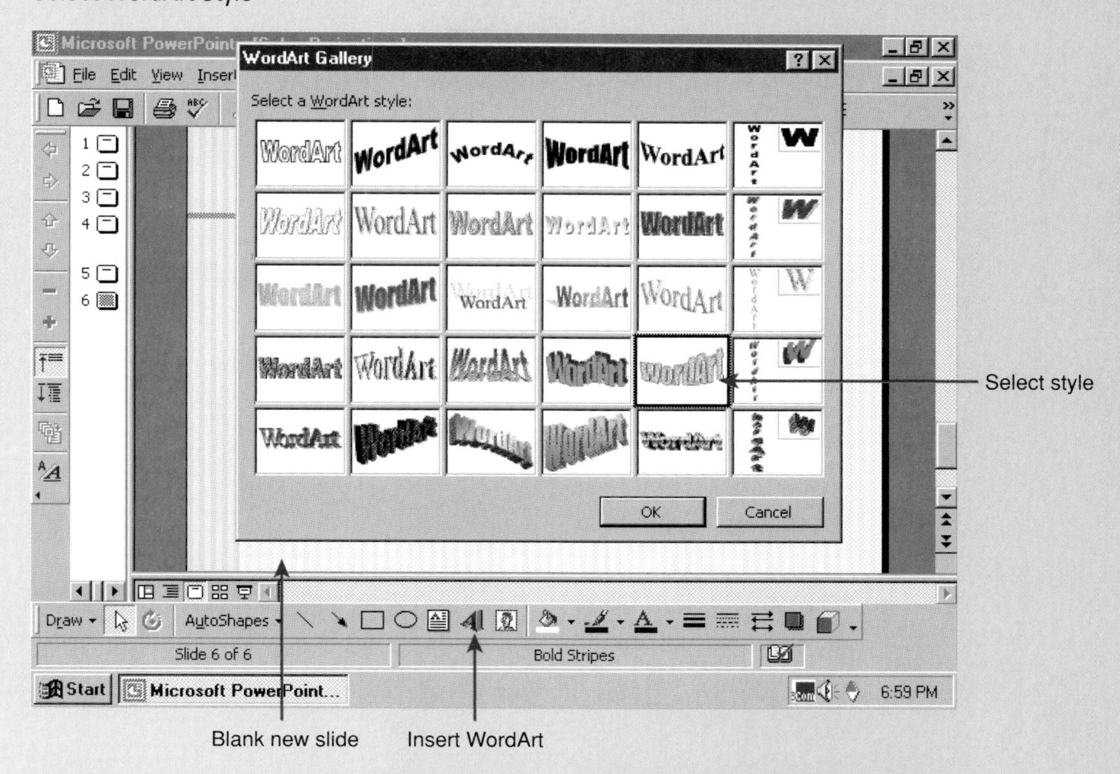

FIGURE 3.18
Edit WordArt Text

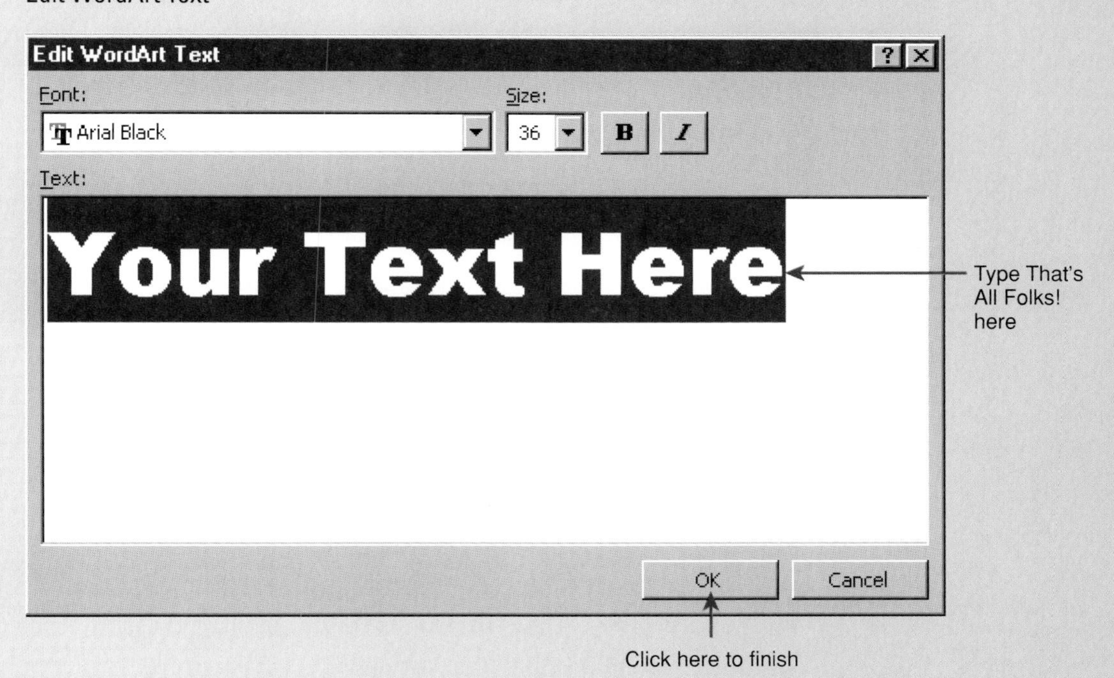

Creating WordArt Text (continued)

6. You should see handles appearing around the WordArt text. Move your pointer to one of the corners. When it changes shape to a **black, two-headed arrow**, left-click and drag to resize the text to match the text in Figure 3.19.

7. To move the text, place your pointer on the text and when it changes to a **black, four-headed** arrow, move to the location as shown in Figure 3.19.

8. **Save** your work. Click **View, Slide Show** to run the Sales Projections presentation and view the different objects you have created in this chapter.

FIGURE 3.19
WordArt Text

Change It!

You can change a WordArt shape rather than apply one of the preformatted styles as you did in this exercise. You can shape the text in a variety of shapes, curves, styles, and color patterns. The WordArt toolbar provides the tools to make stunning effects.

STRENGTHENING YOUR SKILLS

1. In the **Sales Projections** presentation created in this chapter, a Title slide is missing. Create a **new slide** with a title descriptive of the slides. Use the **WordArt** feature to enhance the text on the Title slide. Move the slide to the beginning of the presentation. **Print** the slide.

2. Create a new presentation titled **Buttons and Bows**. Create four slides for this presentation.

   a. For **slide 1**, create a Title slide.

   b. For **slide 2**, create an Organization Chart slide and enter the following data:

      i. Title Placeholder: **Buttons and Bows**

      ii. Susan Thomas, President

      iii. Janice Witherspoon, Assistant to Pres.

      iv. Thomas Wetherly, MIS Manager

      v. Gary Smith, Finance Manager

      vi. Germaine Wilson, Production Manager

   c. **Change font point size to 18** for slide 2 title.

   d. Use the Boxes menu item in the Chart window to change box colors to **green**. (To select all boxes at one time, hold down the Shift key and click each box.)

   e. Select one of the **shadow** styles to add shadows to each box.

   f. For **slide 3**, create a columnar chart slide with the title **First Quarter Sales** and enter the following data:

	July	August	September
East Coast	874	482	982
West Coast	987	645	1,190
Central	452	673	857

   g. Change the **chart type** to one of your choice.

   h. For **slide 4**, create a slide closing the presentation. Use your imagination with either Clip Art, WordArt, or any drawing tools.

   i. **Save** the presentation. **Print it**.

3. You are president of the Business Club at Evergreen College. To thank those members who volunteered their time to community projects, you would like to create a flyer with each of their names. You decide to create the flyer using PowerPoint's Clip Art feature.

   a. Create a new presentation with a **blank slide**.

   b. Select the **Text and Clip Art AutoLayout**.

   c. Double-click the Clip Art placeholder and select the **Academic category**. Select a picture of a **diploma**.

   d. In the slide in the text area, type *In appreciation for all your hard work in*

1998 on behalf of the Business Club.

e. In the **Title** placeholder, type the name of a friend.

f. **Change** one of the colors in the diploma.

g. **Save and print** your work.

4. Re-create the slide as shown in Figure 3.20 using **Clip Art, AutoShapes, and WordArt**. (Two hints: Use the Blank AutoLayout and use the Search for clips feature in the Clip Gallery and type in sailboats.)

FIGURE 3.20

a. To fill AutoShapes with **color**, select the shape, then click the appropriate button on the Drawing toolbar.

b. To add text to this slide, use the **Text Box tool** on the Drawing toolbar. Select the text and change its color by using the appropriate button on the Drawing toolbar.

c. **Save** this slide under its own name and **print** it.

5. Figure 3.21 shows what you can do with the tools available on the Drawing toolbar. You can either re-create this slide or use your own imagination to create your own.

FIGURE 3.21

a. Create a blank slide in any presentation.

b. Click on the **AutoShapes tool** on the Drawing toolbar to display the various shapes. Select a banner shape. Remember, to enter text simply right-click on the shape. Enlarge the banner by clicking on the handle and dragging to resize. To fill the banner and other shapes with color, select the object first, click the **Fill Color** down arrow in the Drawing toolbar. For texture, select the **Fill Color** down arrow, click on **Fill Effects**, **Pattern** and **select a pattern**.

c. The arrows consist of the triangle shape found under **Basic Shapes** in AutoShapes and the **Line tool**. Use the **Free Rotate tool** on the Drawing toolbar to adjust the placement of the triangle shape.

d. Click the **Shadow tool** to add depth to the shapes and the **3-D tool** to add dimension to the rectangle shape.

6. Create a flyer for the Providence Theatre Company that contains the information shown below. You may use either the **AutoContent Wizard**, which includes guidelines for a flyer, or use **AutoLayout**. Let your imagination go and select color or clips to add zip to your flyer.

   Meeting of the Board of Directors

   12:00 noon at the Theatre Room, 2nd floor, Providence Theatre

   Bring a bag lunch and your creative ideas

   If you cannot attend, please contact Susan at 404-299-4021

7. Use the **AutoShapes** to create a card for a special occasion. Use the variety of AutoShapes available in PowerPoint such as **Stars and Banners** and **Basic Shapes** to create an attractive card. For borders, click on **More AutoShapes** under the AutoShapes button. Print out the finished card.

8. PowerPoint provides many tools to enhance the organization chart. Re-create the chart in Figure 3.22. Click Lines in the menu to make lines bolder. Under Boxes, select Shadow, Border Style and Border Color to make the chart appear as the figure or make your own selections. Save your work and print the slide.

FIGURE 3.22

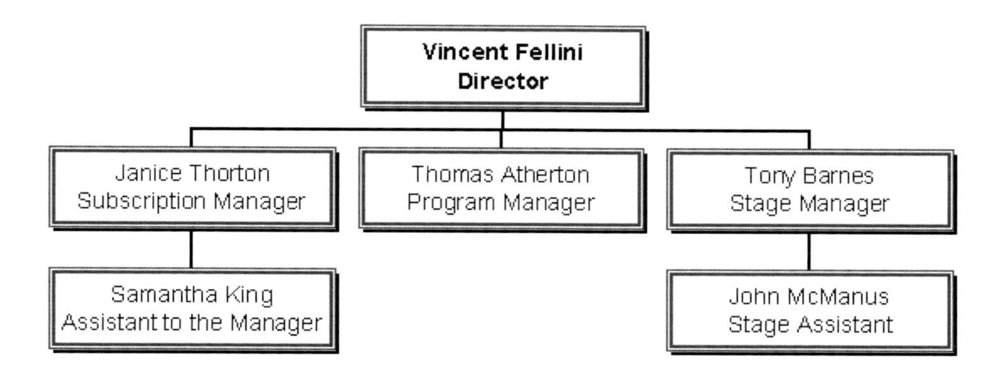

SUMMARY OF FUNCTIONS

TASK	MOUSE/BUTTON	MENU	KEYBOARD
Changing chart type	Click the Chart Type button	Chart, Chart Type	[Alt] C T
Importing an Excel file		Insert, Object, Create from file	[Alt] I O
Inserting a chart	Click Insert Chart button	Insert, Chart	[Alt] I H
Inserting a column	When mouse changes to black arrow to the right of a column, select it and click the Insert Column button	Table, Insert Column	[Alt] A I
Inserting an organization chart	Double-click Organization Chart placeholder in AutoLayout	Insert, Picture, Organization Chart	[Alt] I O
Inserting a picture	Click Insert ClipArt button	Insert, Picture	[Alt] I P
Inserting a table		Insert, Picture, Microsoft Word table	[Alt] I T
Inserting AutoShapes	Click the AutoShap AutoShapes Drawing toolbar	Insert, Picture, Autoshapes	[Alt] I A
Inserting WordArt	Click the WordArt button on the Drawing toolbar	Insert, Picture, WordArt	[Alt] I W

SELF-TEST PROBLEMS

True/False

Circle T for statements that are true and F for statements that are false.

T F **1.** WordArt should be used sparingly because it can clutter a slide if used on more than one word or heading.

T F **2.** Datasheets are objects created only in PowerPoint and cannot be imported.

T F **3.** By default, charts are displayed as columns.

T F **4.** Resizing a chart by dragging on the side handle maintains its proportions.

T F **5.** An Excel worksheet can be edited in PowerPoint.

T F **6.** When an object is embedded, one program is opened inside of another.

T F **7.** Table sizes are limited to four columns or less.

T F **8.** As many pictures as possible should be used on a slide to grab the audience's attention.

T F **9.** Once the Organization Chart is created, you cannot edit its contents.

T F **10.** PowerPoint provides 10 basic AutoShapes to use for drawing purposes.

Multiple Choice

Select the best answer for each question and write the corresponding letter in the blank.

_______ **1.** Which of the following commands begins the process to embed an object in PowerPoint?

- **a.** Select View in the menu and click Master.
- **b.** Click Insert in the menu and select Object.
- **c.** Click File in the menu and select New.
- **d.** None of the above.

_______ **2.** Which of the following steps will insert a blank column in a table?

- **a.** Position the pointer to the left of where you want the new column and select Insert.
- **b.** Double-click the existing column and select New.
- **c.** Position the pointer at the top of the column to the right of where you want the new column and click the Insert Column button.
- **d.** Position the pointer at the top of the column to the right of where you want the new column. When the pointer changes to a black arrow, click to select the column and then click the Insert Column button.

_______ **3.** How do you reposition drawing objects such as arrows and rectangles?

- **a.** Move the pointer over the object and press the Shift key.
- **b.** Move the pointer over the object, click to select, and drag to the new location.
- **c.** Both (a) and (b).
- **d.** Neither (a) nor (b).

_______ **4.** Which of the following is true about organization charts?
- **a.** You should replace the words in the placeholders with your data.
- **b.** To add subordinates, click the subordinate button and then click in the box the subordinates will be connected to.
- **c.** An organization chart is an effective way to visually depict an organization.
- **d.** All of the above.

_______ **5.** Which of the following is true about WordArt?
- **a.** Limit yourself to one WordArt effect per slide to avoid a cluttered look.
- **b.** WordArt provides a gallery of special effects for text.
- **c.** WordArt text can be changed by enlarging, shrinking, or rotating the image.
- **d.** All of the above.

_______ **6.** How is a slide created with a title and graph?
- **a.** Select Slide, New, then select the AutoLayout containing a graph. Double-click the graph placeholder.
- **b.** Select Slide, New, then select Insert in the menu and click Chart.
- **c.** Select Slide, New, then click the Insert Chart button on the Standard toolbar.
- **d.** All of the above.

_______ **7.** Embedded objects can include which of the following?
- **a.** Microsoft Excel spreadsheets
- **b.** A graph
- **c.** Clip art
- **d.** All of the above

_______ **8.** To retain the original proportion of a chart when resizing, which of the following applies?
- **a.** Click the side handle and drag.
- **b.** Click the corner handle and drag.
- **c.** Double-click the chart.
- **d.** None of the above.

_______ **9.** Where can Clip Art be accessed?
- **a.** Clip Gallery
- **b.** Connect to the Web for Additional Clips button
- **c.** Clip Gallery Live
- **d.** All of the above

_______ **10.** What is the difference between a bulleted list and a text box?
- **a.** There is no difference.
- **b.** The text box can be used to annotate charts.
- **c.** The text box is not a placeholder.
- **d.** Both (b) and (c).

Matching

Match each of the elements to the PowerPoint screen shown below with its resulting action.

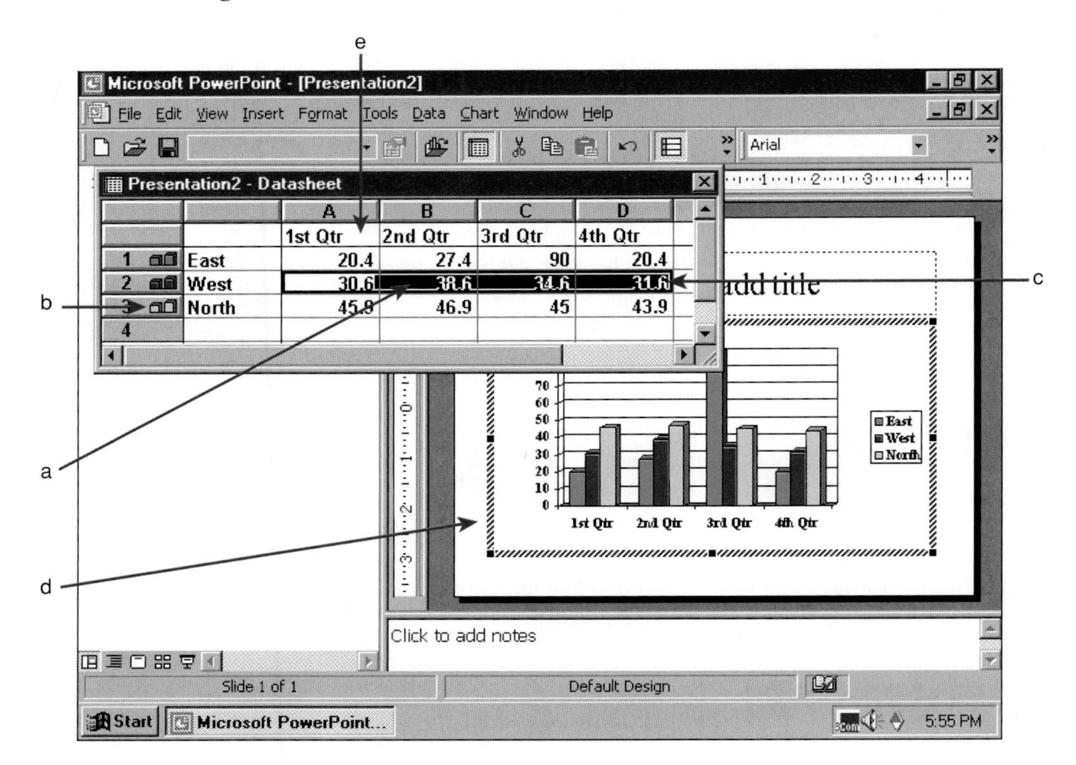

Item	Action
_______	**1.** Enters data to replace the demonstration data
_______	**2.** Points to a column of data
_______	**3.** Indicates the way data are displayed
_______	**4.** Points to a cell with the cell address B3
_______	**5.** Appears after double-clicking the chart placeholder in AutoLayout

Fill in the Blank

Fill in the blank with the missing word or phrase.

1. The ____ button is clicked to insert a table.
2. To create a slide with a placeholder for an organization chart, select the _______ that contains an organization chart.
3. The ____ button centers a title.
4. Click Insert, ____ to begin the process of inserting a picture on a slide.
5. ______, which is found on the Drawing toolbar, provides already categorized shapes.
6. Data are displayed in either of two views: a _____ or a _____.
7. The ____ menu choice contains the Chart command.
8. The _____ toolbar contains the Insert WordArt button to add special effects to text.

9. Once a picture is selected and the Picture toolbar appears, the _____ ______ button allows you to replace color.
10. To select a layout that is clear of all objects, the ____ format would be chosen.

ANSWERS

True/False: 1. T 2. F 3. T 4. F 5. T 6. T 7. F 8. F 9. F 10. F

Multiple Choice: 1. b 2. d 3. b 4. a 5. d 6. d 7. d 8. b 9. d 10. d

Matching: 1. c 2. e 3. d 4. a 5. b

Fill in the Blank: 1. Insert Table 2. AutoLayout 3. Center 4. Picture 5. AutoShapes 6. datasheet, chart 7. Insert 8. Drawing 9. Recolor Picture 10. Blank

Making a Presentation Dynamic

OUTLINE

LEARNING OBJECTIVES

After completing this chapter, you will be able to

- Add slide transitions
- Add animation to text
- Insert and play movie clips
- Hide slides
- Use the Meeting Minder
- Create hyperlinks to link with different objects
- Create and view a Web page

Adding Transitions between Slides

Special effects make a presentation more lively and diverting to an audience. In the steps below, you will learn how to create transitions between slides and avoid a totally linear look to your presentation.

1. Open the file **chap4-1** and save it as **A Guide to Effective Presentations**.
2. You should be at **slide 1** in Normal view. Click the **Slide view button** to change views. Click Slide Show in the menu and select **Slide Transition.**
3. Click the Effect drop-down list arrow and select **Checkerboard Across.**
4. Click **Slow** for the speed. Then click **Medium** to see the difference. Leave the setting at Medium as shown in Figure 4.1.

(continued on page 134)

FIGURE 4.1
Slide Transition Dialog Box

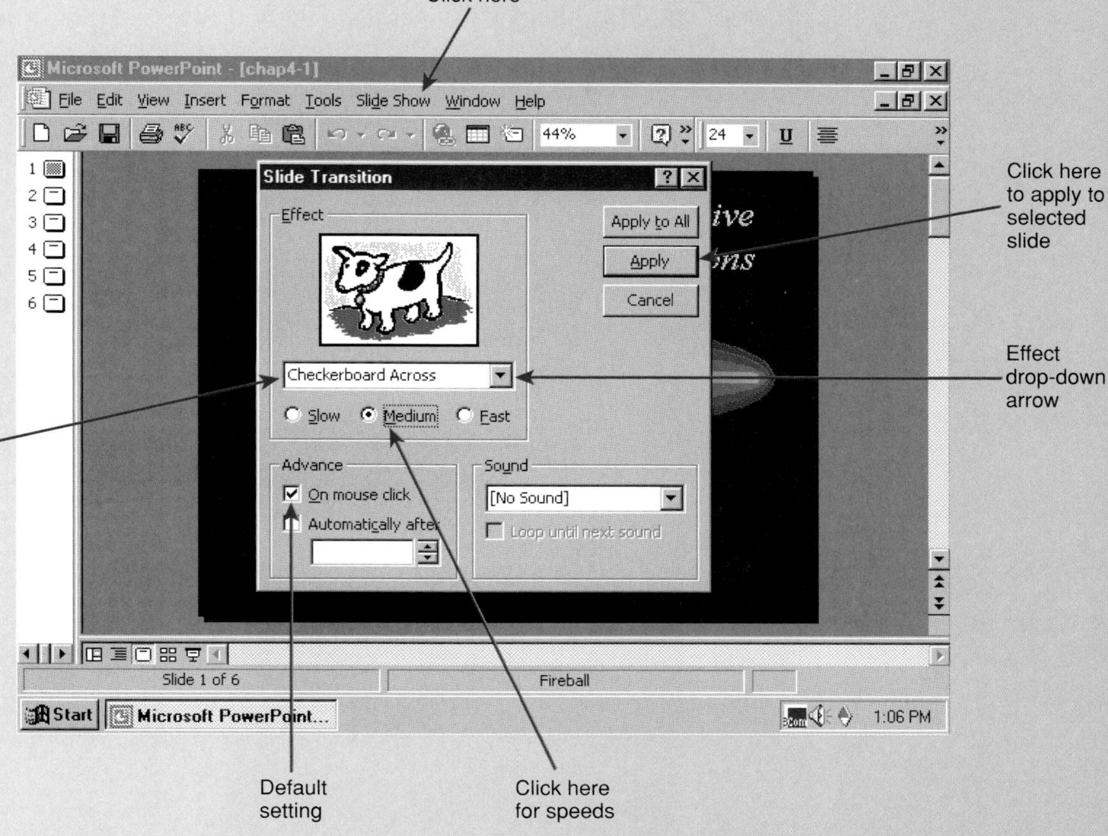

TIP

Sound Effects

PowerPoint includes a selection of sounds in the Slide Transition dialog box. Click the Sound drop-down list arrow to choose a sound effect to go with the transition.

NOTES

Design Issues

Make sure the transitions you use emphasize your points, not draw the audience's attention to the special effects. To avoid this, set transitions at a speed that moves your presentation along.

Adding Transitions between Slides (continued)

5. Click **Apply** to set this transition for only the **Title Slide**.

6. Click the **Slide Show button** at the bottom left-hand corner of your screen to view the transition for slide 1.

7. Press the **Esc key** to exit the Show. Go to **Slide Sorter view** to view all slides on a single screen. Click **slide 2** and then hold the **Shift key** and click **Slides 3–6.** A thin black line appears around each of the slides, indicating that they are selected. Refer to Figure 4.2 for reference.

8. Click **Slide Show, Slide Transition** and select **Fade Through Black**. The speed should be set to **Fast.** Click the **Apply button**. As an option, you can select the **Slide Transition Effects button** on the Slide Sorter toolbar. Refer to Figure 4.2 for guidance.

9. You can see the effect again by clicking the **Slide Transition icon** at the bottom of any transition slide. Run the show by selecting **Slide Show, View Show.**

10. **Save** your file to wherever your student files are stored.

FIGURE 4.2
Transitions in Slide Sorter View

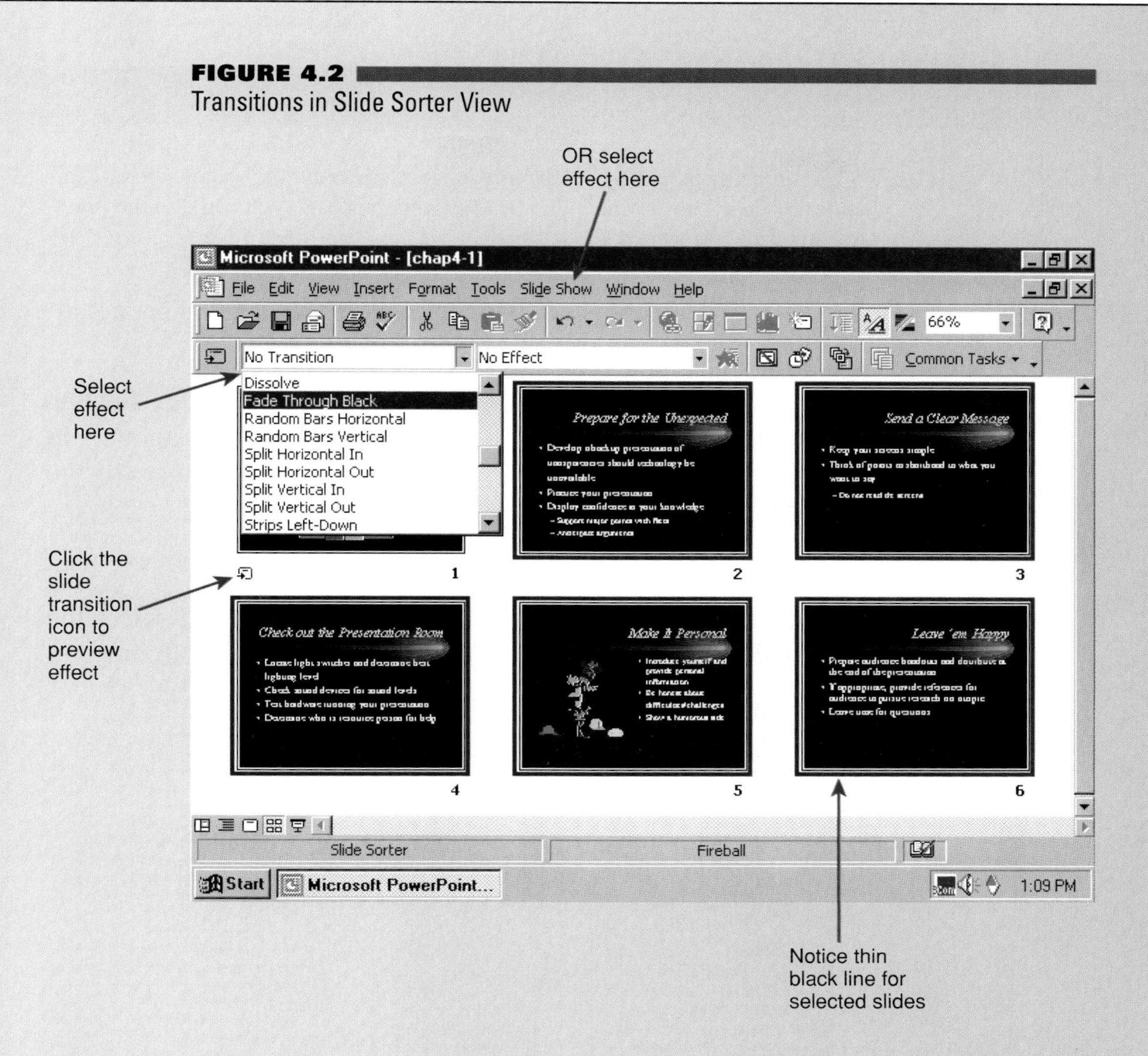

Adding Animation to Text

You can animate text by controlling its appearance on the screen, either character by character or line by line. Once a line appears, you can dim the previous lines to focus the audience's attention.

1. Open the file **A Guide to Effective Presentations** if you are not already there. You should be in **Slide view**.
2. Go to slide 2. Click **Slide Show** in the menu and click **Custom Animation**. Click **Text 2** as the first item you wish to animate in the **Check to animate slide objects box**. Text 2 moves to the Animation order box as shown in Figure 4.3.
3. Click the **Effects tab**. Leave the default setting **Fly From Left**.
4. Click the **After animation drop-down list arrow** and select the **gray color** so that after the bullet is selected, it will be dimmed.

(continued on page 138)

FIGURE 4.3
Timing for Custom Animation

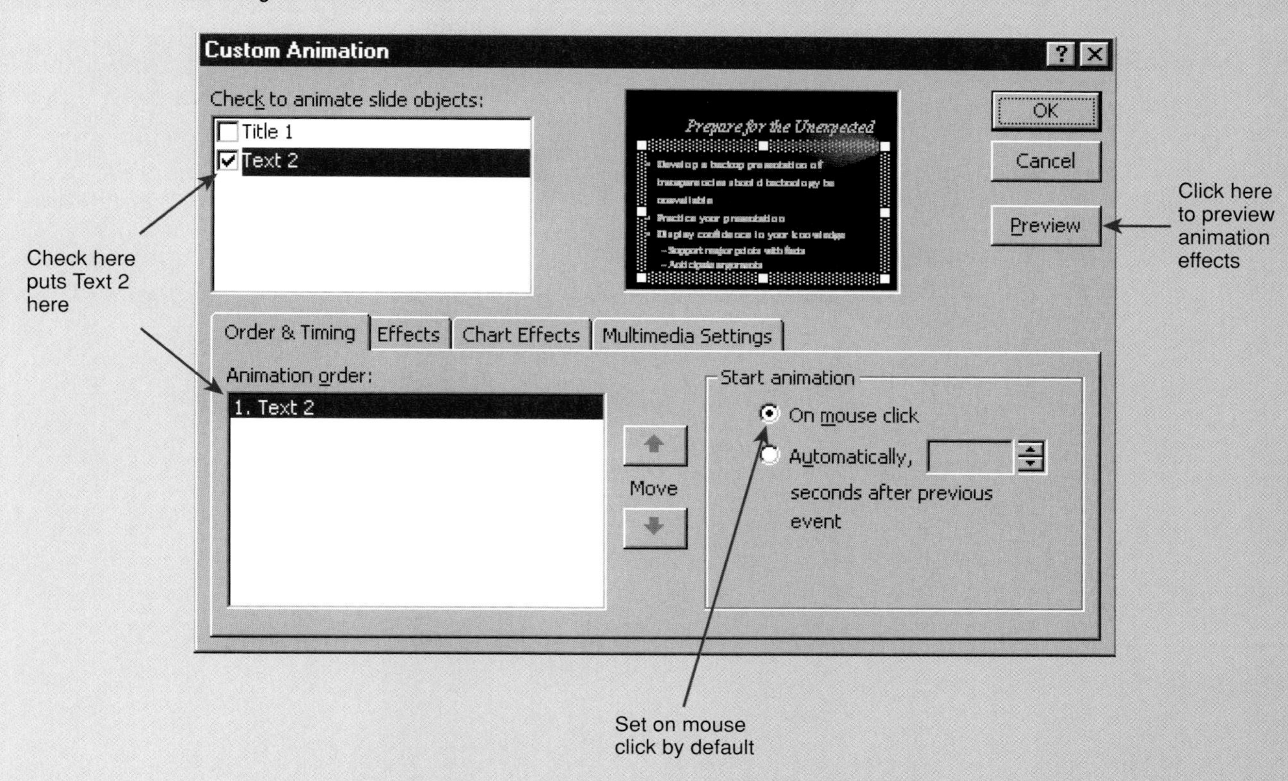

NOTES

Specialized Animations

For text, you can introduce text one character or one word at a time. For charts, you can introduce a chart series or chart categories, one by one. The animations can appear when you click them or after a particular period of time.

TIP

Preset Animation

To quickly animate an object, select it on the slide, then open the Slide Show menu. Select Preset Animation and make your choice. Many of these preset animations contain sounds.

Adding Animation to Text (continued)

5 Click the **Grouped by drop-down arrow** and select **2nd** so that you animate sub-bullets separately. Refer to Figure 4.4 for guidance. Click the **Preview button**. Click **OK** to return to slide 2.

6 Click the **Slide Show button** to view the animation effects on slide 2. (Remember to click the mouse button to activate the bullets.) Press the **Esc key** to return to **Slide view**.

7 **Save** your work.

FIGURE 4.4
Effects for Custom Animation

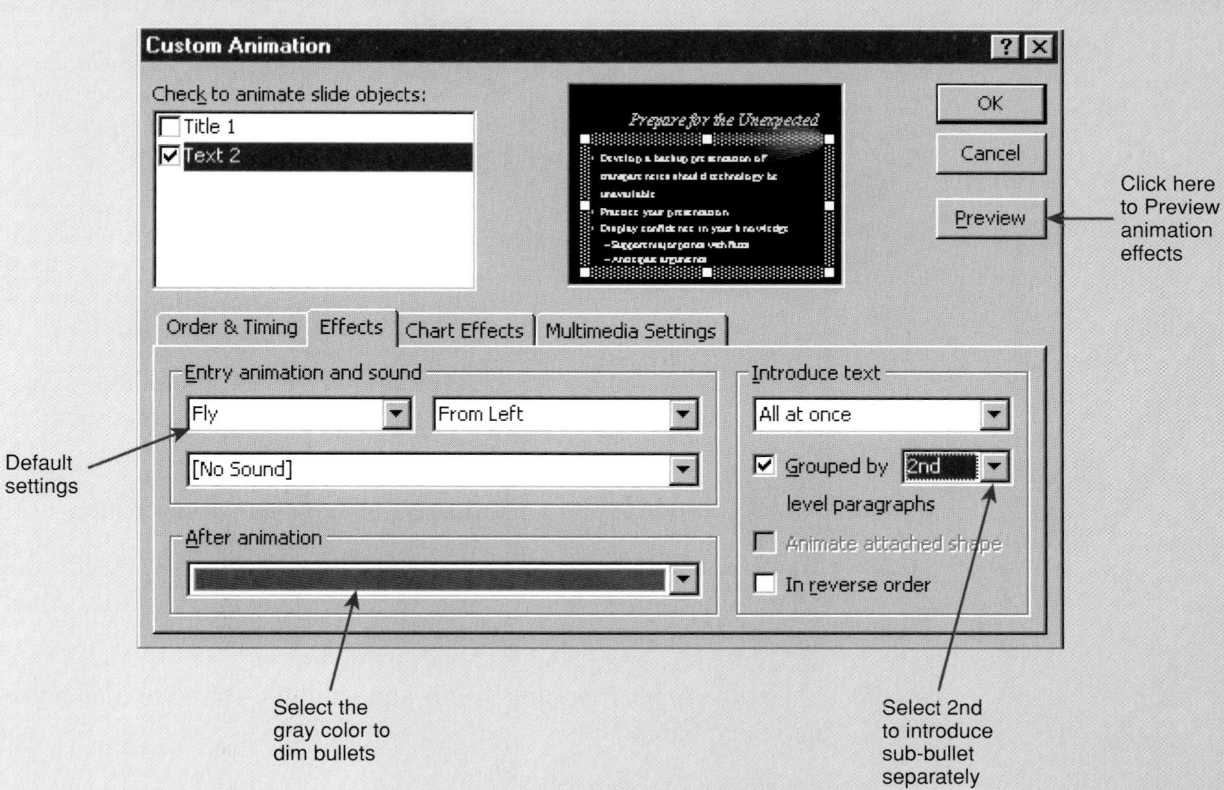

Using Sound in a Presentation

In this lesson, you will learn to insert sound on your slides. You can insert sound that you activate yourself or insert a sound connected to a slide transition. (You won't be able to hear the sounds unless your computer is equipped with a sound card and speakers.)

1. Make sure **A Guide to Effective Presentations** file in PowerPoint is open.
2. Go to **slide 5** of your presentation. You should be in Slide view.
3. Select **Insert** in the menu. Select **Movies and Sounds**. Click **Sound from Gallery**. The file dialog box appears as shown in Figure 4.5.
4. Type **Applause** in the Search for Clips text box. Press Enter.
5. Click on the **Horn and Cheers** file. Click Insert Clip. Click the Close button ☒. (If your software doesn't contain this file, select another sound file.)
6. A window appears asking you if you want the sound to play automatically. Click No.

(continued on page 142)

FIGURE 4.5
Insert Sound

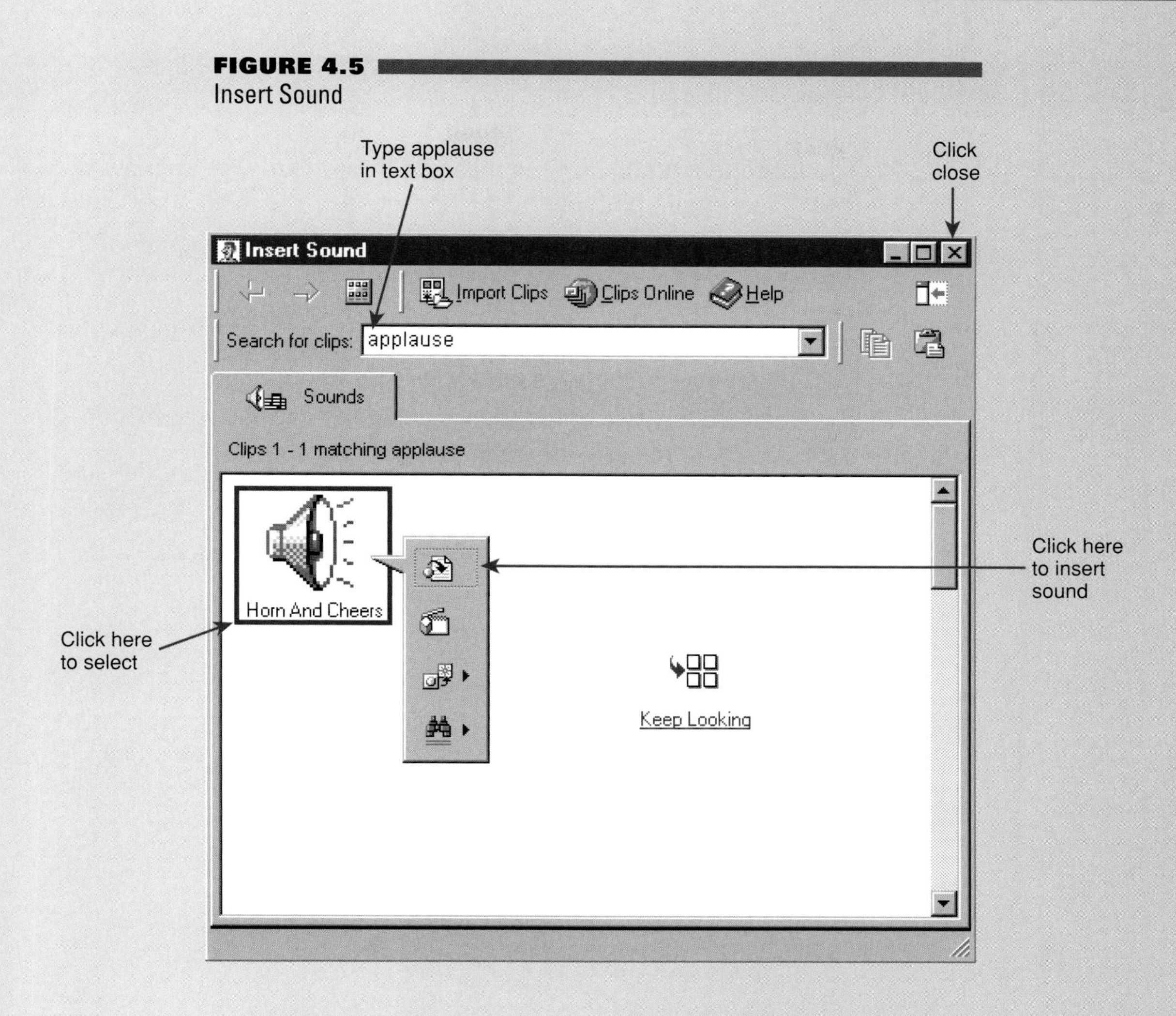

Not Too Much Sound

The same applies to sound as has already been mentioned with other special effects. An occasional sound may gain the attention of your audience but do not overwhelm them. You will detract from the message of your presentation.

Using Sound in a Presentation (continued)

7. The **Applause icon** should appear on the screen with sizing handles. Place your pointer on the icon and when it changes to a black four-headed arrow, hold your pointer and move to the bottom left side of your slide. Refer to Figure 4.6 for placement.

8. Click the **Slide Show view button**, and then click the icon to start the sound effect.

9. Go to **slide 6**. Select **Slide Show** in the menu, **Slide Transition**.

10. Click the Sound drop-down arrow and select **Chime**. Click the **Apply** button to finish. Click the **Slide Show button** to hear the sound effect. Press **Esc** to return to **Slide view**.

11. **Save** your work. **Close** the file.

FYI PowerPoint provides additional sources for sounds. Select Insert in the menu and click Movies and Sounds, Sound from File. Open the Media folder in the Windows folder to select a sound.

FIGURE 4.6
Sound Icon

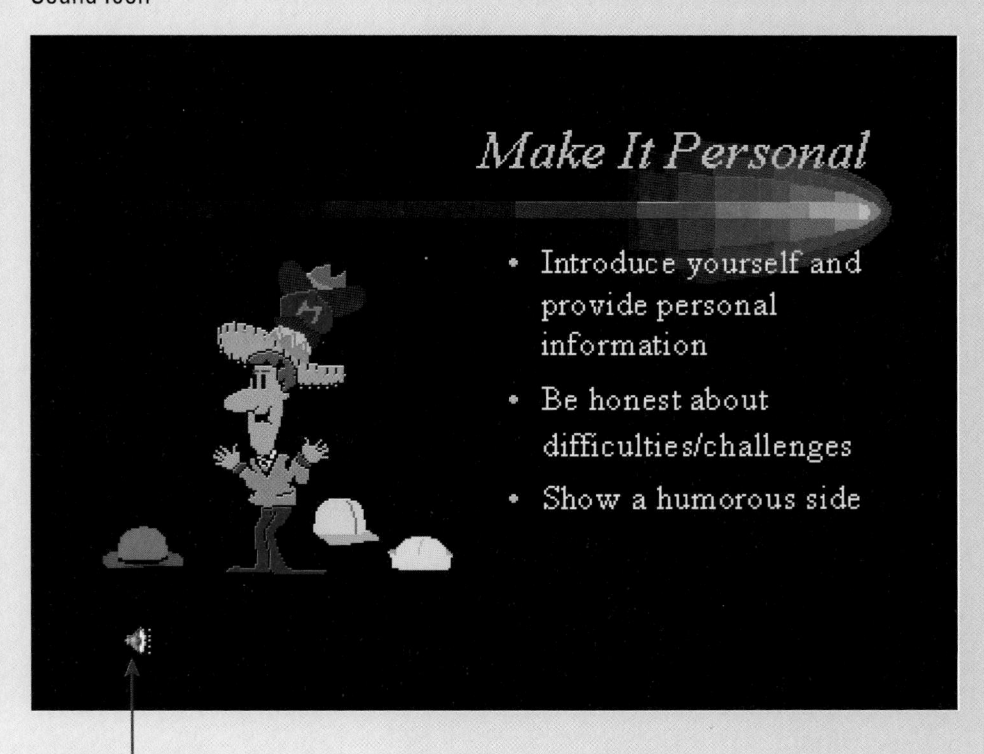

Icon moved to bottom left corner. Click on icon to start sound effect.

Inserting and Playing Movie Clips

In the following steps, you will learn how to insert movie clips in a presentation. The movie clip becomes an object that can be resized, moved, or deleted like other objects.

1. Open the file **chap4-2**. **Save** the file as **Trans-World Air** so that the original file remains unchanged. Click to Slide View.
2. Select **Insert, Movies and Sounds, Movie from file**. Your movie file, **winner.avi**, is located wherever your student files are stored. Select the file from the files listed and click **OK**.
3. A window appears asking you if you want the movie to play automatically. Click No. The movie is inserted by displaying its first frame. You can drag it so that it appears in the location as shown in Figure 4.7.
4. **Resize** the movie to enlarge it by dragging any selection handle.
5. Double-click the object to **play** the movie.
6. To **edit** the movie, right-click the movie icon. **Click Edit Movie Object**.

(continued on page 146)

FIGURE 4.7
Movie Clip

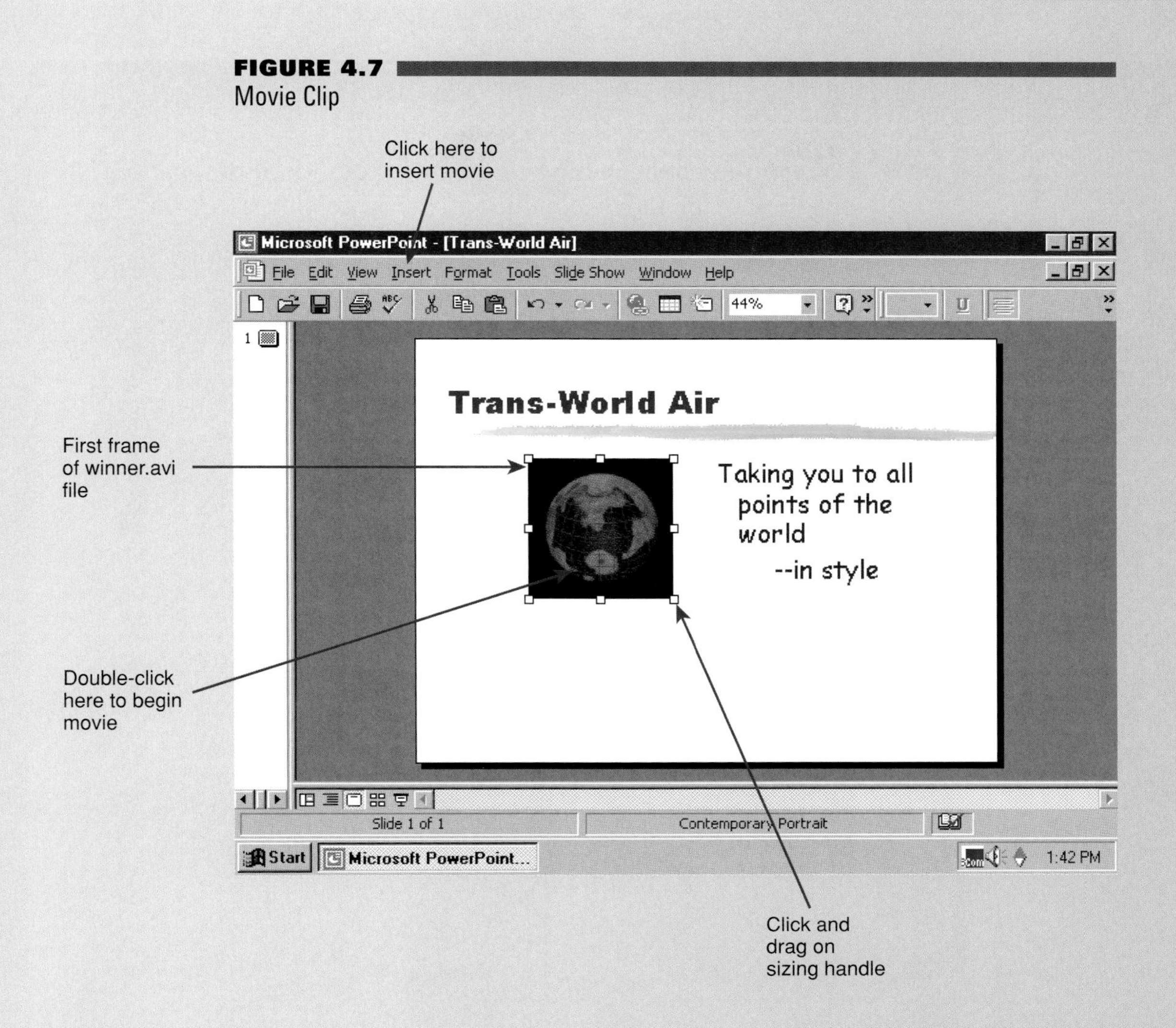

Where's the Movie?

You can set a movie or sound to play automatically at certain times in a presentation. Select Slide Show, Custom Animation and click the Order and Timing tab to set the timing.

Inserting and Playing Movie Clips (continued)

7. **Change** the movie settings. Click the **Loop Until Stopped** check box to play the movie continuously (Figure 4.8). Click **OK**.
8. Double-click the movie to **play**. Double-click again to **stop** the movie.
9. **Save** your work.

FIGURE 4.8
Play Options

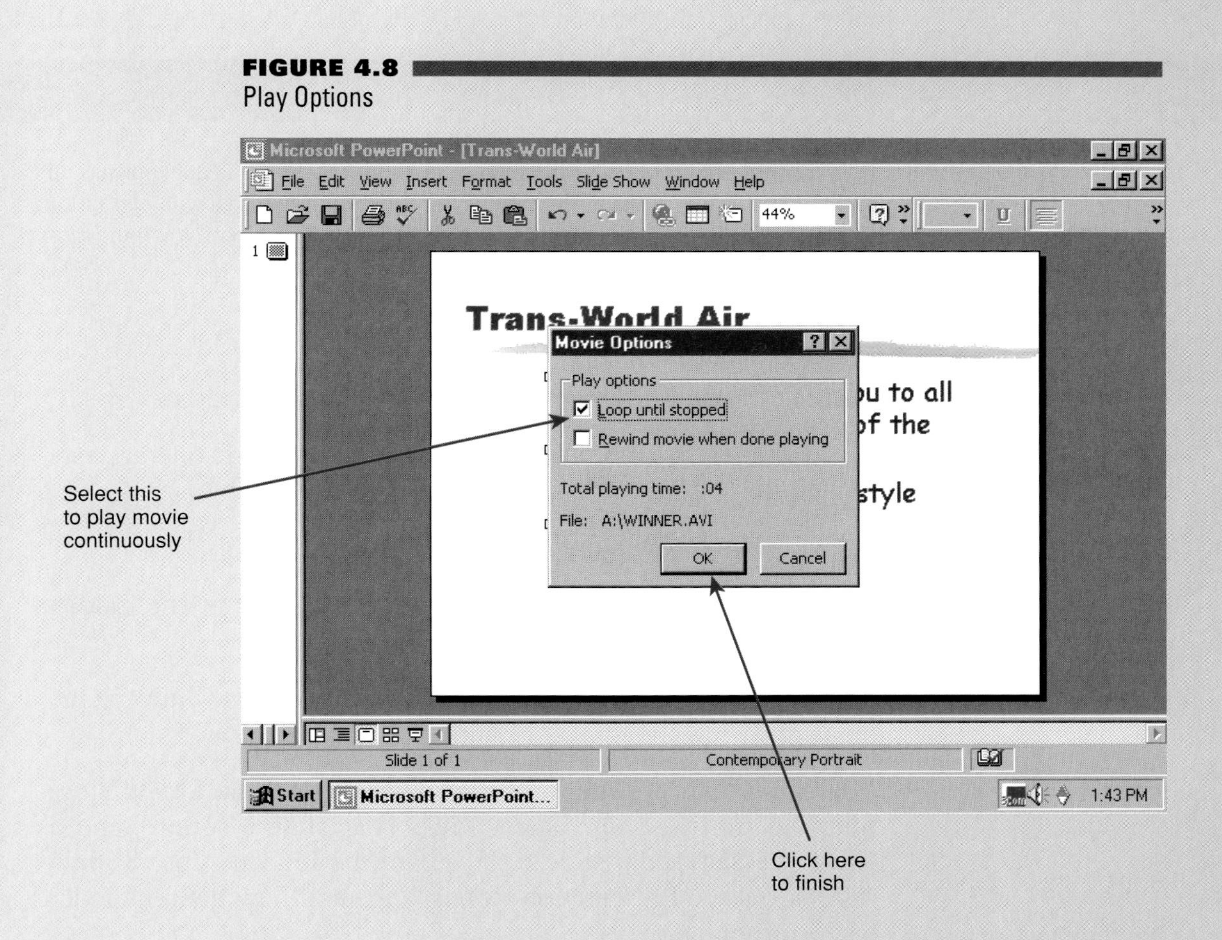

Using Hidden Slides

During a presentation, you may decide that a particular slide is not appropriate for the audience. You have the option of hiding slides so that you can tailor your message even as you are speaking. In the following steps, you will learn how to hide a slide.

1. Open the file **A Guide to Effective Presentations**.
2. Click the **Slide Sorter view button** to switch views.
3. To hide **slide 4**, click the slide to select it. A dark line appears around the slide as shown in Figure 4.9.
4. Select **Slide Show** in the menu and click **Hide Slide**.
5. Notice a slash appears through the slide number of the hidden slide.
6. Begin the slide show by selecting **Slide Show, View Show** in the menu and view the impact of hiding a slide.
7. You can unhide a slide during a show. Click **Slide Show, View Show** to run the show again. Press **H** at **slide 3** (titled Send a Clear Message), the slide right before the hidden slide. **Slide 4** (Check out the Presentation Room) appears. View the remainder of the presentation.
8. **Save** your work.

FYI While developing a presentation, if you decide to unhide a previously hidden slide, simply select **Slide Show** and click **Hide Slide**. This turns off the Hide Slide function.

FIGURE 4.9
A Hidden Slide

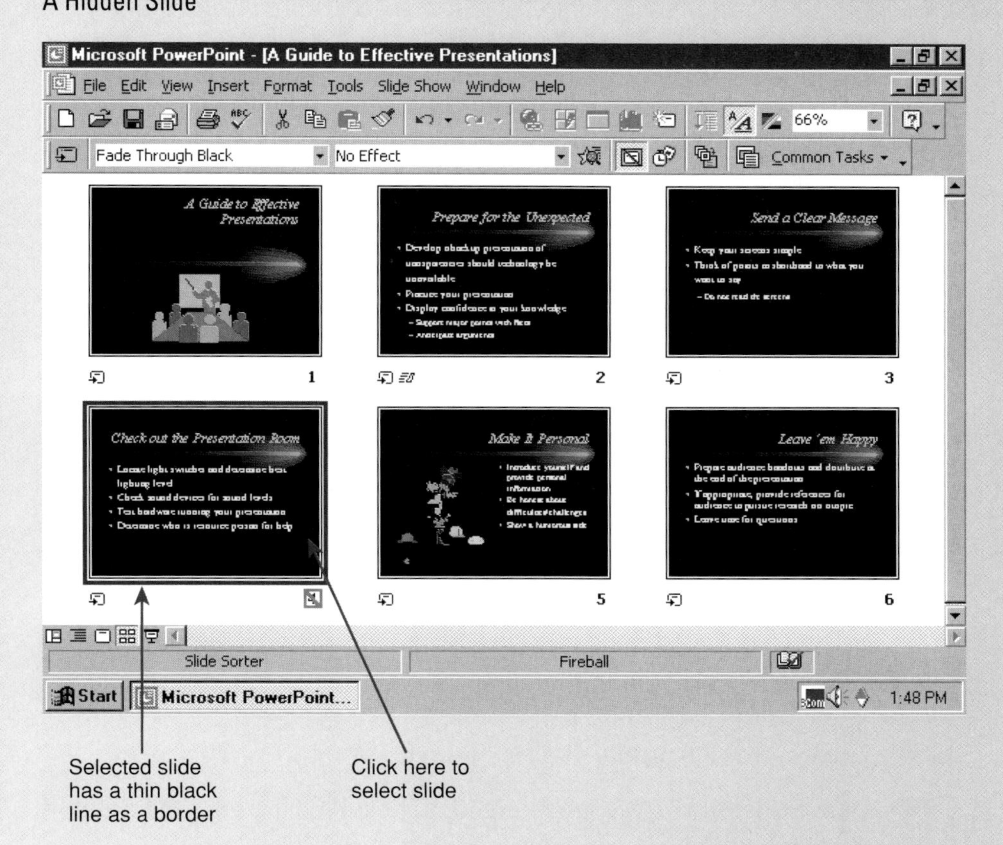

TIP

More about Hiding/Unhiding Slides

You can unhide a slide wherever you are during a show, not merely at the slide before the hidden slide. Right-click for a shortcut menu, select Go, Slide Navigator and select the hidden slide.

Working with the Meeting Minder

During or after a presentation, the audience often makes comments or suggestions that you might like to record. Meeting Minder is a PowerPoint feature that lets you jot down messages to yourself, even during a presentation. Follow the steps below to practice working with this feature.

1. If you are not in **A Guide to Effective Presentations** file, **open** the file now. Go to **slide 6**. You will attach a comment to this slide.
2. Select **Tools** in the menu, and click **Meeting Minder**.
3. Click the **Action Items tab**.
4. In the **Description box**, type **Look for video clips that convey happiness**. Refer to Figure 4.10 as a guide.
5. Click in the **Assigned To** box, and type **Me**.
6. Change the **Due Date** to **10/3/99**. Click **Add** to add the item.
7. In the **Description box**, type **Make presentation slides available on the Internet**.
8. Click in the **Assigned To box** and type **Me**.
9. Leave the **Due Date** unchanged. Click **Add** to add the second item. Click **OK**.
10. Action items appear at the end of your presentation on a new slide. Click the **Slide Show button** to **run** the presentation and view the items. Compare your last slide to Figure 4.11.
11. Return to **Slide view** and **Save** your work.

FIGURE 4.10
Meeting Minder

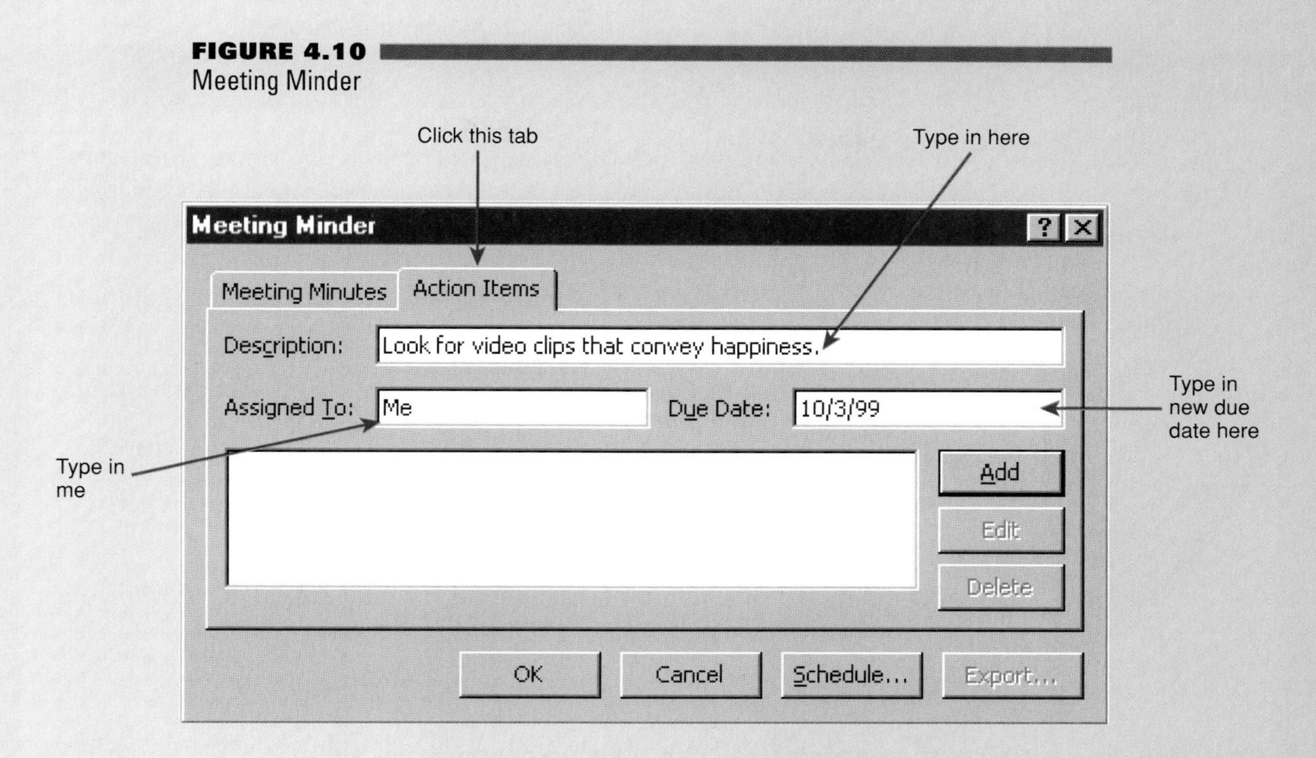

FIGURE 4.11
Action Items

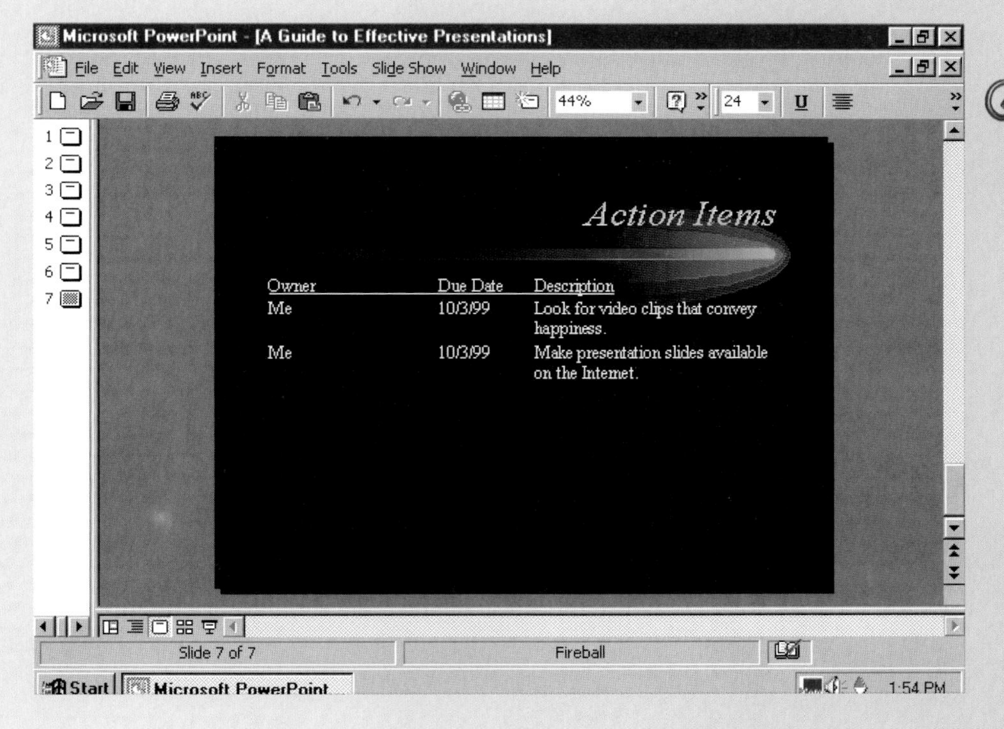

TIP

Taking the Meeting Minder to Microsoft Word

You can print your minutes and action items. Click **Export** in the Meeting Minder dialog box. If not already selected, click **Send Meeting Minutes and Action Items to Microsoft Word**. Click **Export Now** to move your items to Word. Your items are now in a Word document and as such can be edited or printed.

Adding Hyperlinks

When an object on one slide is associated in some way with another, you can create a hyperlink that allows you to move between the two objects during a presentation.

1. Open the file **Trans-World Air**. If you did not complete the tutorial that created this file, open the original file, **chap4-2**.
2. Right-click the word **World** on the screen. Select **Action Settings**.
3. Click the **Hyperlink to** option and click the drop-down arrow.
4. Click **Other PowerPoint Presentation** from the list of hyperlinks as shown in Figure 4.12.
5. Click the presentation **Caribbean Holiday** stored wherever your student files are located. Click **OK**.
6. Click slide 1 as shown in Figure 4.13.
7. Click **OK** to save the hyperlink. Click **OK** to close the Action Settings dialog box. **Save** the changes to the **Trans-World Air** presentation.
8. **Run** the Trans-World Air presentation and click the **hyperlink** to test. The hyperlink is shown in colored and underlined text. You should link to the **Sailing in the Caribbean** slide.

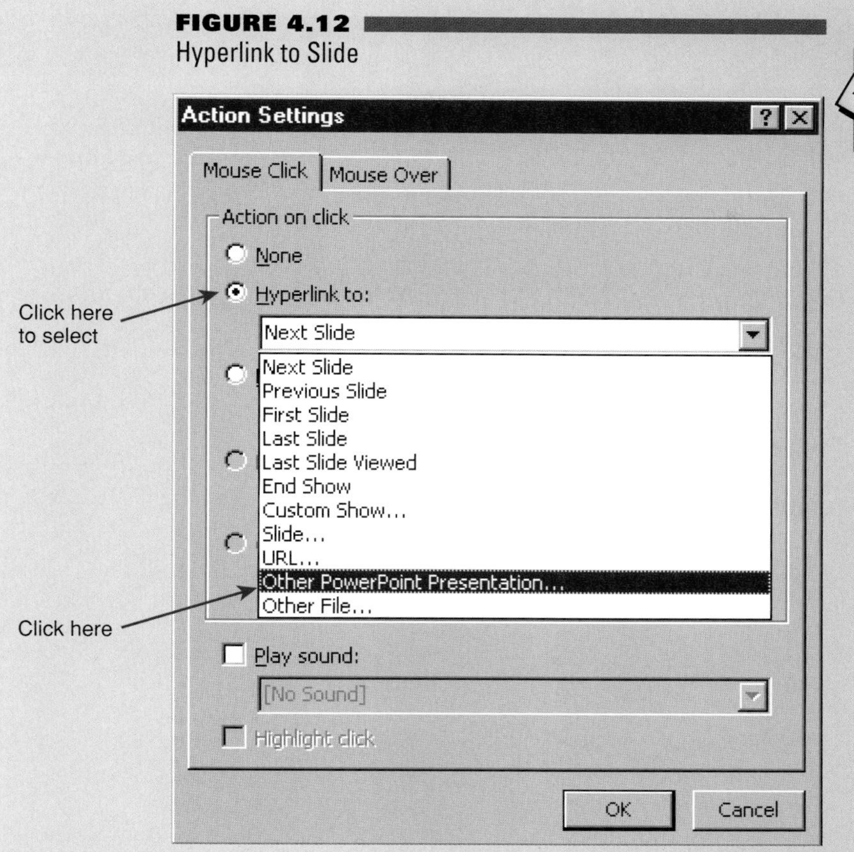

FIGURE 4.12
Hyperlink to Slide

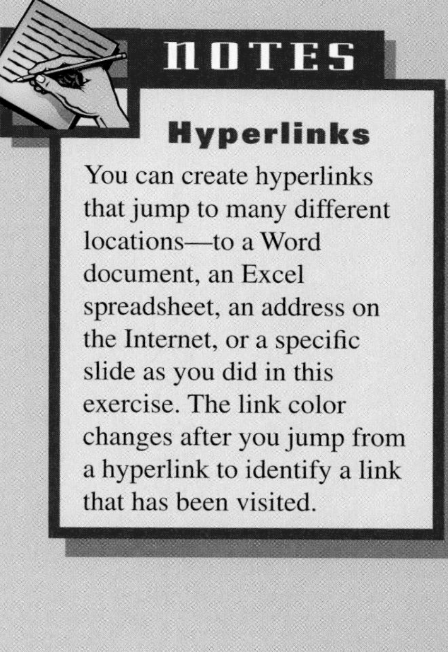

FIGURE 4.13
Action Settings

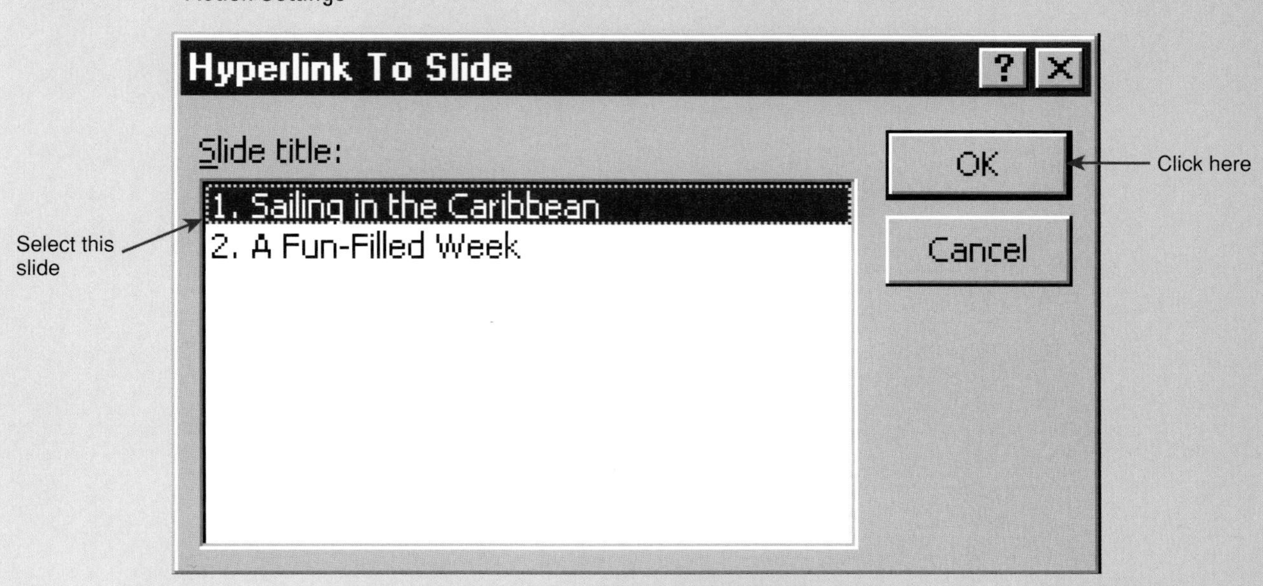

Creating and Viewing a Web Page

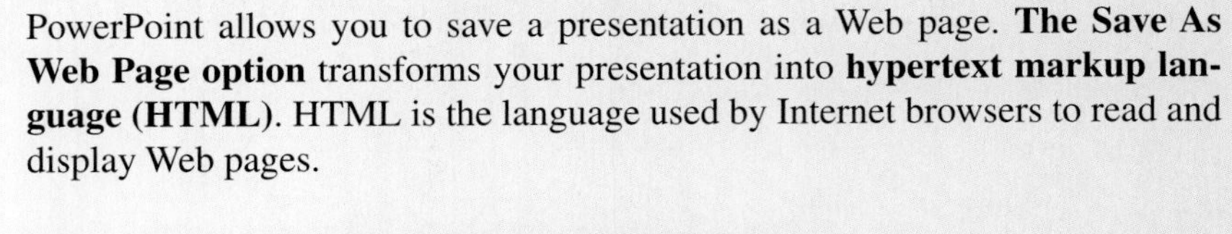

PowerPoint allows you to save a presentation as a Web page. **The Save As Web Page option** transforms your presentation into **hypertext markup language (HTML)**. HTML is the language used by Internet browsers to read and display Web pages.

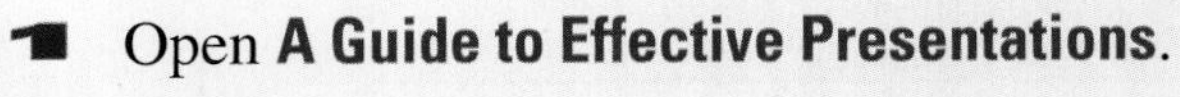

1. Open **A Guide to Effective Presentations**.
2. Select **File** in the menu, and click **Save as Web Page**.
3. Click the **Change title** button (Figure 4.14) and type **Effective Presentations**. Click OK.

(continued on page 156)

FIGURE 4.14
Convert to HTML

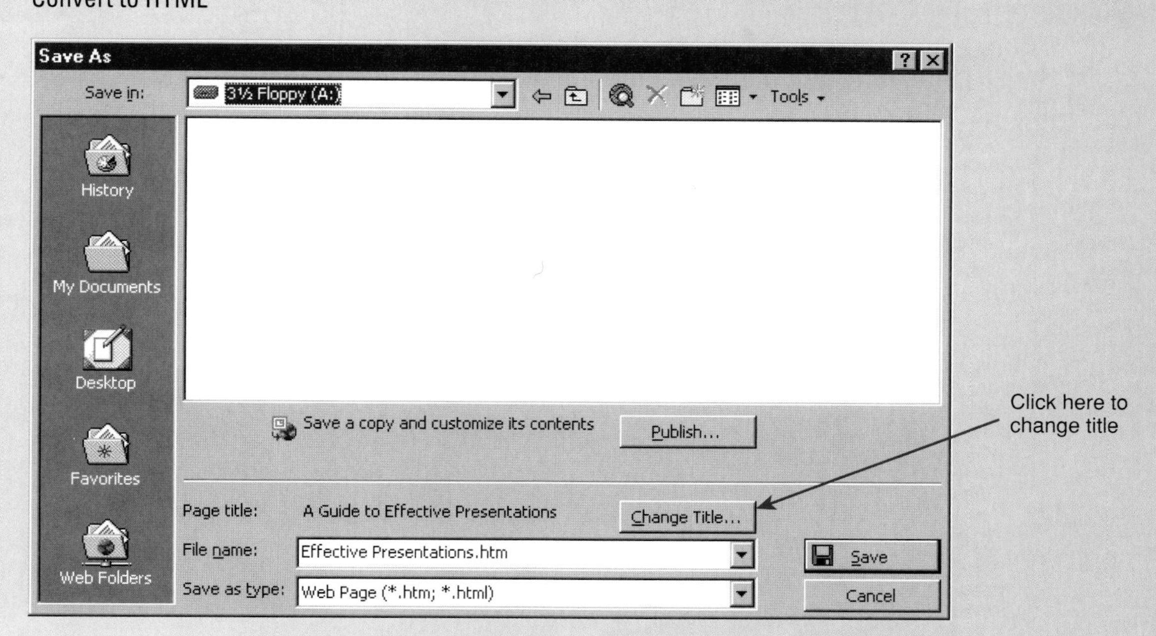

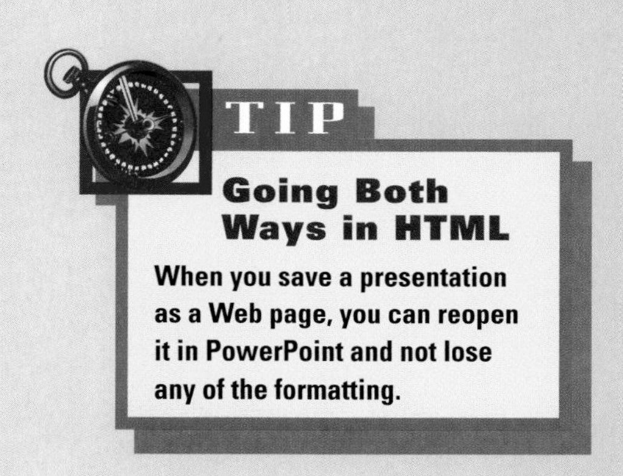

Creating and Viewing a Web Page (continued)

4. Click the **Save** button in the dialog box.
5. Select **File, Web Page Preview** in the menu to view the presentation as a Web page. Figure 4.15 shows the PowerPoint presentation as a Web page. Notice the outline pane is converted to a table of contents to help with navigation.

FIGURE 4.15

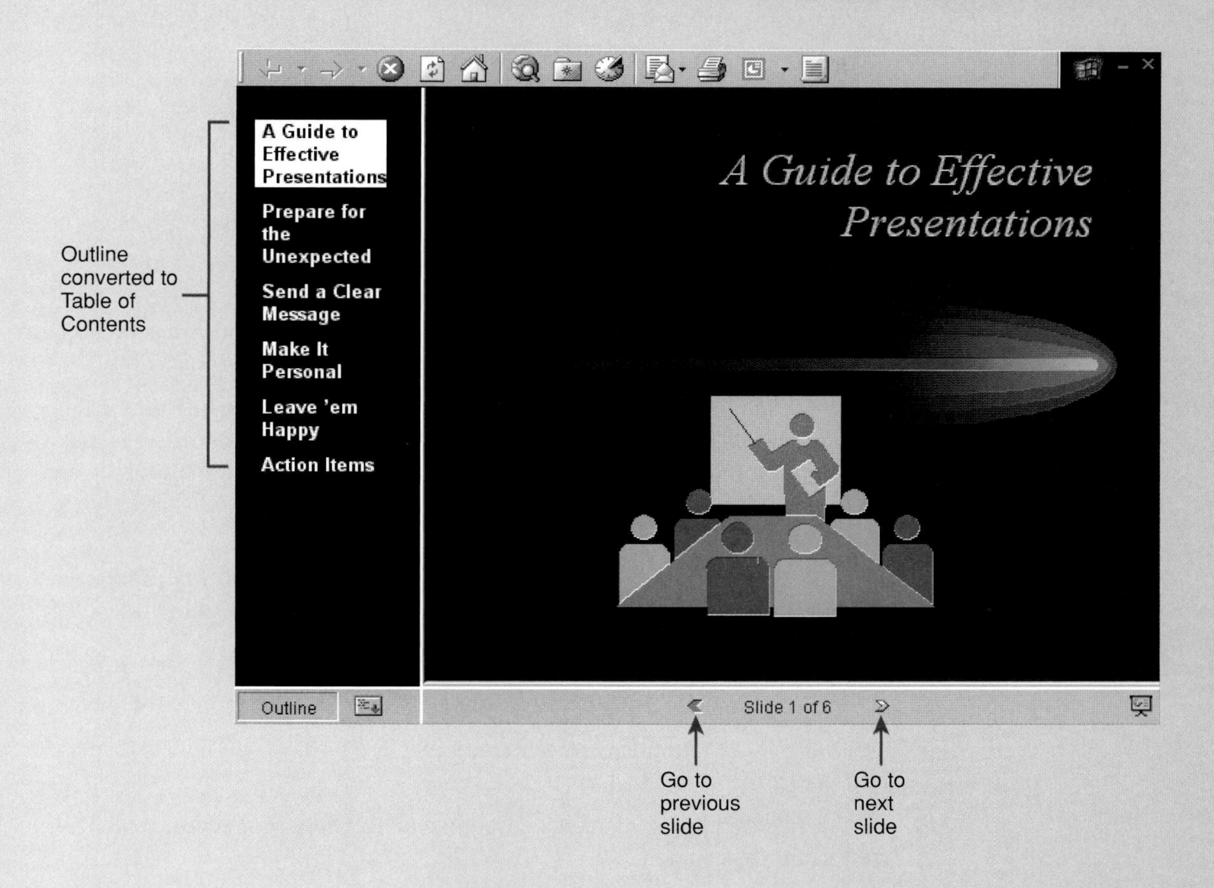

The Web Toolbar

The Web toolbar allows you to access a Web search page, send mail or Web pages and store favorite sites, among other options.

STRENGTHENING YOUR SKILLS

1. Open the file **chap4-3** on your student disk. Save the file as *Security Issues* so that the original file remains unchanged. Make the changes to the slides as described below. Begin at Slide Sorter view.
   a. At **slide 1**, the title slide, select **Box Out** for the slide transition. Set the transition for **medium speed**. Select **Laser** as the slide transition sound.
   b. Select all slides by selecting **Edit, Select All**. **Deselect slide 1** by holding the Shift key and clicking slide 1. Select **Blinds, Vertical** for the slide transition for the remaining slides in the presentation. Select a **slow speed** for transition.
   c. Go to **slide 3** and select Slide view. Select the placeholder for the title. (You must always select the placeholder before you create Preset Animation.) Click Slide Show in the menu bar and select **Preset Animation**. Select the **Drop In** effect for the title of slide 2. Select the placeholder for the bulleted list and give it the **Appear** effect.
   d. Continue in Slide view and go to **slide 2**. Apply **Custom Animation** to **Text 2** on this slide.
   e. For effects, select the **Fly from Bottom—Left** option.
   f. Select a **color** in the **After animation drop-down box**, to dim a previous bullet.
   g. In the Introduce Text area, select **Grouped by 2nd** to have sub-bullets display separately.
   h. Create a **hyperlink** from the bullet **Enforcement of Proper Procedures** to **slide 4** in the same presentation.
   i. **Save** your work and select Slide Show to see the impact of your special effects and test your hyperlink.
2. Open the file **chap4-4** and rename the file *Million Dollar Mistakes.*
   a. Insert Clip Art for **slides 2**, **4** and **13** that will enhance the message of the slide. You also may replace existing clips on other slides with those of your choosing.
   b. Select a sound from the **Gallery** for **slide 1**. Do not set it to play automatically.
   c. Set a slide transition for all the slides. Run the presentation to view the impact of the clip art, transitions and sound.
   d. Go to **slide 9**. After selecting **Meeting Minder** under **Tools** in the menu, click on **Action Items** and insert the following in the dialog box:

      Description: Research case studies and provide Internet sites

      Assigned to: B. Barnett

      Due Date: 12/12/99

      Export your notes to a Microsoft Word document and print them.
   e. Hide **slide 11**. Run your presentation to see the impact of hiding the slide. Run the presentation again and unhide the slide.
   f. Save the presentation as a Web document. Select the **Web Preview** menu choice to preview your presentation on the Web.

3. In Chapter 3, you created a presentation titled *Sales Projections.* Open the file and enhance the presentation by adding slide transitions and custom animations of your choice. Run the presentation to view your show.

4. In the **Strengthening Your Skills** section at the end of Chapter 3, you created a presentation titled *Buttons and Bows.* Open the presentation and insert multimedia effects such as slide transitions and custom animation to enliven the slide show. Run the show to see the impact of your work.

5. Create hyperlinks in a slide show to link slides. Open **chap4-5** and save the file as *Computer Devices.* The title slide displays four subtitles. Link the bullet Input Devices to **slide 2**. Link the bullet Output Devices to **slide 3**. Link the bullet Storage Devices to **slide 4**. Provide a link back to **slide 1** for each of the slides. Run the presentation and test your links.

6. Controlling your slide presentation in a confidential manner is important. Open the slide show, *Million Dollar Mistakes*, to practice controlling the slide show without the shortcut menu appearing on screen.

    a. Begin the slide show.

    b. Press **F1** to display the list of keyboard shortcut commands, then press **Enter** to clear the screen.

    c. Press **N** to proceed to the next slide, **slide 2**.

    d. Go to **slide 7** by pressing 7 and enter.

    e. Press **Ctrl + P** to activate the annotation pen. The pen is a handy tool that allows you to enter information on a slide with freehand drawing. At **slide 7**, circle the word anything to place emphasis on it. Press **Esc** or **Ctrl + A** to show the arrow.

    f. Press **Esc** to end the show.

SUMMARY OF FUNCTIONS

TASK	MOUSE/BUTTON	MENU	KEYBOARD
Animating objects	Click Animation Effects button	Slide Show, Custom Animation, or Preset Animation	[Alt] D, M, or P
Converting to Web pages		File, Save As Web Page	[Alt] F
Hiding a slide	Hide Slide button on Slide Sorter toolbar	Slide Show, Hide Slide	[Alt] D H
Adding a hyperlink	Select placeholder and then click Insert Hyperlink button	Insert, Hyperlink; or Slide Show, Action Settings	[Ctrl] K
Inserting Movies		Insert, Movies and Sounds, Movie from File, or Movie from Gallery	[Alt] I V, F, or M
Inserting Sounds	Slide Transition button on Slide Sorter toolbar	Insert, Movies and Sounds, Sound from File, or Sound from Gallery	[Alt] I V, N, or S
Using Meeting Minder		Tools, Meeting Minder	[Alt] T T
Previewing a presentation on the Web		File, Web Page Preview	
Adding transitions	Slide Transition button on Slide Sorter toolbar	Slide Show, Slide Transition	[Alt] D T
Unhiding a slide	Hide Slide button on Slide Sorter toolbar	Slide Show, Hide Slide	[Alt] D H

SELF-TEST PROBLEMS

True/False

Circle T for statements that are true and F for statements that are false.

T F 1. The Slide Transition icon is located in the Slide Sorter view.

T F 2. Custom animation is found under Edit in the menu.

T F 3. Sub-bullets must be displayed at the same time as the main bullets.

T F 4. Animating text refers to controlling its appearance on the screen.

T F 5. Set transitions at a slow speed so that the audience's attention is drawn to the special effects.

T F 6. Charts can be animated series by series.

T F 7. Sounds can only be activated by the presenter.

T F 8. Once a presentation is saved as a Web page, the outline pane becomes a table of contents.

T F 9. PowerPoint provides only clip art and animation effects to enliven a presentation.

T F 10. Once a slide is hidden you cannot unhide that slide.

Multiple Choice

Select the best answer for each question and write the corresponding letter in the blank.

______ **1.** Transitions include which of the following?
- **a.** Cut Through Black
- **b.** Dissolve
- **c.** Checkerboard Across
- **d.** All of the above

______ **2.** To which of the following can a transition effect be applied?
- **a.** To a single slide
- **b.** To all slides in a presentation
- **c.** Both (a) and (b)
- **d.** Neither (a) nor (b)

______ **3.** What menu selection begins the process of displaying a PowerPoint presentation on the Web?
- **a.** File, Save
- **b.** Insert, Hyperlink
- **c.** File, Save As Web Page
- **d.** None of the above

______ **4.** Which is untrue about movies?
- **a.** You are restricted to displaying the movie in its original size.
- **b.** To edit a movie, right-click the object.
- **c.** You can change the movie setting to loop continuously.
- **d.** By default, a movie must be clicked to begin.

______ **5.** Which of the following is true about hidden slides?
- **a.** Pressing the H key at the slide following a hidden slide will unhide the slide.
- **b.** Hiding slides is a feature available only when you are designing your presentation.
- **c.** One way to see which slide is hidden is by looking at the Slide Navigator.
- **d.** None of the above.

______ **6.** The Meeting Minder includes which of the following features?
- **a.** It records meeting minutes and miscellaneous comments.
- **b.** It can be exported to Microsoft Word so that the items can be inserted into a document or printed.
- **c.** It can record the name of the person responsible for a task and the due date.
- **d.** All of the above.

______ **7.** Which of these locations can be linked by a hyperlink in PowerPoint?
- **a.** Word document
- **b.** Excel spreadsheet
- **c.** Another slide
- **d.** All of the above

______ **8.** What steps permit insertion of sounds?
- **a.** Insert, Movies and Sounds, Sound From File.
- **b.** Tools, Sounds, Insert.
- **c.** Insert, Movies and Sounds, Sound From Gallery.
- **d.** Both a and c.

_______ **9.** What objects are available on the Web toolbar?

- **a.** Favorites
- **b.** Search
- **c.** Mail
- **d.** All of the above

_______ **10.** Which of the following is true about the Slide Sorter view?

- **a.** Transition effects can be applied to only one slide.
- **b.** Hidden slides are not identified in this view.
- **c.** Several slides can be selected at once by holding the Shift key and clicking the slides.
- **d.** Slide transition effects cannot be previewed.

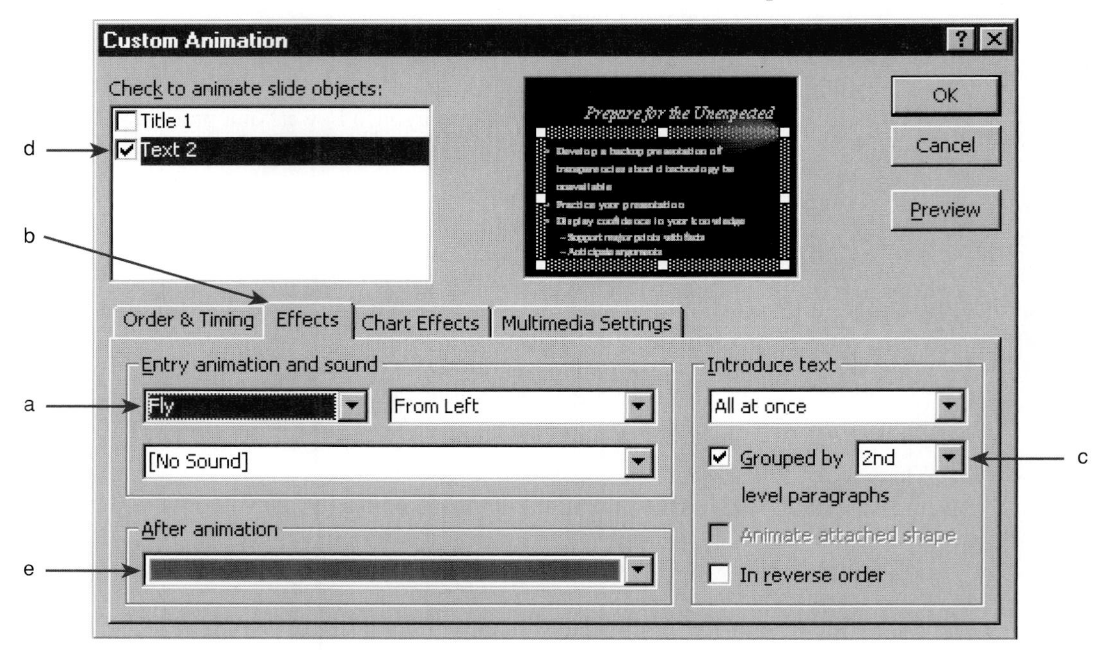

Matching

Match each of the elements to the PowerPoint screen shown above with its resulting action.

Item	Action
_______	**1.** Displays options for various animation features
_______	**2.** Changes text color for dimmed text
_______	**3.** Identifies item selected for animation
_______	**4.** Selects an animation effect
_______	**5.** Sets sub-bullets to display separately

Fill in the Blank

Fill in the blank with the missing word or phrase.

1. Press _______ on the keyboard to unhide a slide during a presentation.
2. The _______ _______ is a feature that records minutes or messages.
3. A(n) _______ allows movement directly from one slide to another object.
4. _______ is the language used to create home pages.

5. After visiting a link, the hyperlink changes its ______.
6. The Save As ______ ______ begins the process of transforming a presentation into a Web page.
7. When a bullet is ______, its color changes and it becomes less noticeable on the screen.
8. One way to add text and a picture is to select the ______ ______ AutoLayout.
9. An example of a ______ is Fade Through Black.
10. In ______ ______ View, click the Slide Transition icon to preview a transition effect.

ANSWERS

True/False: 1. T 2. F 3. F 4. T 5. F 6. T 7. F 8. T 9. F 10. F

Multiple Choice: 1. d 2. c 3. c 4. a 5. c 6. d 7. d 8. d 9. d 10. c

Matching: 1. b 2. e 3. d 4. a 5. c

Fill in the Blank: 1. h 2. Meeting Minder 3. hyperlink 4. HTML 5. color 6. Web Page 7. dimmed 8. Text & Clip Art 9. transition 10. Slide Sorter

INDEX

Notes

Notes

Notes